THE ESSENTIAL
FUNDRAISER'S HANDBOOK

THE ESSENTIAL
FUNDRAISER'S HANDBOOK

A Guide to Maximizing Donations, Retaining Donors,
and Saving the Giving Sector for Good

LISA GREER

XENO

Book design by Mark E. Cull

Library of Congress Cataloging-in-Publication Data

Names: Greer, Lisa, 1958– author.
Title: The essential fundraiser's handbook: a guide to maximizing donations, retaining donors, and saving the giving sector for good / Lisa Greer.
Description: First edition. | [Pasadena, California]: Xeno, [2024] | Includes bibliographical references and index.
Identifiers: LCCN 2023047033 | ISBN 9781939096159 (trade paperback) | ISBN 9781939096166 (ebook)
Subjects: LCSH: Fund raising.
Classification: LCC HG177 .G767 2024 | DDC 658.15/224—dc23/eng/20231102
LC record available at https://lccn.loc.gov/2023047033

The National Endowment for the Arts, the Los Angeles County Arts Commission, the Ahmanson Foundation, the Dwight Stuart Youth Fund, the Max Factor Family Foundation, the Pasadena Tournament of Roses Foundation, the Pasadena Arts & Culture Commission and the City of Pasadena Cultural Affairs Division, the City of Los Angeles Department of Cultural Affairs, the Audrey & Sydney Irmas Charitable Foundation, the Meta & George Rosenberg Foundation, the Albert and Elaine Borchard Foundation, the Adams Family Foundation, Amazon Literary Partnership, the Sam Francis Foundation, and the Mara W. Breech Foundation partially support Red Hen Press.

First Edition
Published by Red Hen Press / Xeno Books
www.redhen.org

ACKNOWLEDGMENTS

It's likely news to no one that a book like this—or any book, I'm guessing—doesn't come together without a whole lot of help from a whole lot of people. This book is no exception.

When my first book, *Philanthropy Revolution*, was published, I had no expectations as to what the response would be. I was—and continue to be—astonished and thrilled that a movement I wanted to create has actually become a "thing."

Shockingly, I was, and still am, the only major donor who has decided to make "Saving Giving" their mission. Maybe that's due to the huge undertaking required to create and move a mission forward. (I think it's probably good that I was initially a bit naïve about that.) Between writing, traveling, speaking engagements, endless webinars, and constant interaction with fundraisers (throughout the world) who want to do better, I've been on one of the most exciting and invigorating rides I ever imagined.

I am so thankful that my family and friends have been patient with me in adapting to this obsession. I am so grateful to all of them, and you all know who you are. Thanks for understanding and supporting me throughout these past years.

To my amazing husband, Josh, you know I couldn't do any of this without you. Thanks for humoring (and supporting) my need to continue hosting our salons and fundraisers and to keep our lives under control when I'm on incessant Zoom calls. Thanks for continuing to be my biggest fan and support system. To my kids—thanks for putting up with the late nights and loads of people in and out of the house at our events—especially on school nights. Thanks also for all you do to make the world a better place, whether its creating or running nonprofits, advocating for change, being a thought partner, or editing my newsletters. I'm so proud of all of you.

Also on the family side, thank you to Cousin Tamara and my brother Steve Zola, for your support, guidance, and for all you do to make fundraising better.

To my dear friend Larissa, thanks for being my partner in the first book, and for guiding me on this book.

To Stephanie, I am so grateful to have found you! I should have known that partnering with amazing, erudite Canadian women was the way to go. You've gone above and beyond and I so appreciate it.

To all the staff at Red Hen Press, thanks for taking this project on and for being so supportive. Kate—it's such a gift to have met you and to count you as one of my friends. To Mark, Tobi, Rebeccah, Shelby, and the rest of the team, I appreciate you all so much. It's truly incredible to watch a nonprofit publishing house continue to be so successful.

To Brooke, you know that I couldn't have gotten through this without your patience, understanding, good humor, and support. I'm forever grateful for our years working together.

Andrea—thanks for keeping cheerful amid the turmoil. You're been a great addition to our team.

One of the most gratifying and surprising things about this experience has been the hundreds of dedicated fundraisers I've met (or e-met!) from all over the world. When I received my first letters and email from people in Canada and Australia and Israel and Germany who had read the book, it was surprising and exciting. When I received the one from a fundraiser in Sri Lanka, I was truly bowled over. The content of these emails, and the wide range and huge numbers of professional fundraisers (at all levels) who tell me that I've changed the way they fundraise is beyond gratifying. It turns out that, as I had imagined but wasn't certain of, loads of professional fundraisers and nonprofit leaders have known that the system needed to be changed for some time. It's now clear that my presence on the scene—especially and specifically because I've been a major donor—gave many fundraisers the confidence to know that other people recognized the need as well, and they weren't alone. I love hearing the success stories from fundraisers who've used my concepts and methodology to make their organizations more sustainable—and also to help them enjoy and appreciate their choice to work in this sector.

Some of my biggest supporters in the sector have been there for years now, and they have been thought partners and cheerleaders, and many have become close friends. I'm talking to you, Kassie Cosgrove, Tim Sarrantonio, Adam Friedman, Daisy Banks, Connor Adams, Nathan Chappell, Beth Breeze, Greg Warner, Brian Gawor, Claire Axelrad, Katie Lord, Holly Miori, Sami Zoss, Andrew Olsen, and my very first "superfan," Rory Traynor. If I've forgotten someone on that list, please forgive me. You are all brave changemakers and warriors on this path to "saving the giving sector for good." I appreciate you all so much.

CONTENTS

IT'S A TEAM SPORT

THE FUTURE IS BRIGHT

FOREWORD

By Dr. Beth Breeze
Director, Center for Philanthropy, University of Kent, UK

As Jane Austen almost wrote: It is a truth universally acknowledged that a nonprofit in possession of an important mission must be in want of individual donors. Yet, despite the essential role private individuals play in supporting every type of nonprofit activity across the world, our understanding of what these donors need and want—and, just as crucially, what they don't want—in order to gain and sustain their support is often sadly lacking. The collective value of donations from individuals far outstrips the value of funding from corporations and philanthropic foundations (collectively known as "institutional donors") by a ratio of three to one, yet these latter sources of voluntary income get far more attention from scholars, practitioners, and the general public. This is partly for practical reasons: institutional donors may only provide around a quarter of total nonprofit funding, but they create a paper trail that makes them much easier to find, to quantify, to study, and to pass comment on. They might have a website, issue press releases, and have staff with easily accessible contact details. Institutional donors are often keen to be visible because their motivation includes achieving business benefits or securing legitimacy and the right to operate. Such is the domination of institutional philanthropy in the public imagination that when philanthropy is being discussed—and especially when it is being criticized—what commentators and critics usually have in mind is foundations and corporations, not individuals.

Yet it is people who contribute three-quarters of all donations and therefore bear the greater burden and kudos for keeping good causes in business. Individual donations mostly come from living donors, whilst legacies written by people into their wills are constituting a growing share of total donated income. Surely, then, understanding the perspective of those making gifts today and those pledging them for the future is crucial for all fundraisers and nonprofit leaders? Yet the actions, experiences, desires, and bugbears of individual donors are much harder to grasp than those of institutional donors. There is no easy way to identify generous people, no convenient database or public record listing all individual donors that can be analyzed and surveyed. Many people are keenly private and prefer not to discuss their giving (or to "virtue signal," as the critics would have it), and most are too busy getting on with their lives—working, socializing, raising their families—to have time to offer their insights on what it feels like to be a donor in addition to donating their hard cash.

As an academic who studies philanthropy, the absence of the individual-donor perspective in discussions about the health and future of the nonprofit sector has long bothered me. How can we understand acts of giving without meaningful insights from those who give, and how can we improve fundraising without factoring in the experiences of those who are on the receiving end of fundraising communications and activities? The individual-donor community is, of course, not the only important perspective—thankfully, great strides have been made in recent years to bring the beneficiary perspective front and center. Serving beneficiaries is, of course, the reason nonprofits exist. But nonprofits cannot fulfill their missions if they cannot pay the rent, utility bills, staff salaries, volunteer expenses, and governance costs. Donors matter because nonprofits cannot run on goodwill alone.

So I was delighted to encounter Lisa Greer's writing, in which she clearly, passionately, and often humorously conveys the individual-donor perspective. Lisa's experience is especially interesting because she landed on the potential-major-donor radar overnight when the startup operated by her husband and a friend became a successful, publicly listed company. Coming to the sudden attention of fundraisers in every organization she had a connection with (and plenty she did not) allowed her a unique opportunity to share what it feels like to be at the center of fundraisers' hopes, and to convey constructively and empathically what does and does not land well when fundraisers try to reach potential donors. Lisa's voice is worth listening to because she is a generous giver—she pledged her first $1 million donation before her husband and friend rang the ceremonial bell at the New York Stock Exchange—and she is now a full-time philanthropist and advocate for better fundraising. We need to listen when she recounts what it is like to be on the receiving end of large quantities of badly worded asks and misjudged solicitations, because she is sharing these accounts in order to help nonprofits learn from those mistakes and do better.

We live in a time of multiple, simultaneous crises, including the climate emergency, ongoing social and racial injustice, war in Europe, and inadequate progress toward the Sustainable Development Goals. In the face of these immense global challenges, and in light of the ongoing quotidian needs in every community to improve local facilities and ensure everyone has a chance to meet their potential, we need more—not less—philanthropy. This means we also need more skilled and successful fundraisers who understand how to find and inspire donors, how to build meaningful and sincere relationships with them, and how to provide an accessible and enjoyable opportunity to use private wealth for public good.

Lisa's willingness to help this work be done better, despite her personal needs for privacy and time spent with loved ones, is a testament to her commitment to improving fundraising so that nonprofits can thrive and make a bigger positive difference in the world. Lisa's insights have helped me and my students to better understand and relate to individual donors, and I'm sure this new book will prove equally valuable to all who care about the health and impact of the philanthropy sector.

INTRODUCTION

My mission is simple: to save giving.

Why?

I believe the work nonprofits do, in general, is critically important for the millions of people and programs they serve (and, in turn, the world). I also believe research, in general, doesn't lie. Research has shown an ongoing decline of donors and fundraising revenue over the last decade. Each time new statistics are released, the nonprofit industry seems shocked, but it's clear to me and others that a comprehensive "reboot" of the way we do fundraising is in order (in fact, it's past due). Fundraising is the engine that keeps nonprofits running. However, I hear again and again that fundraisers don't know what to do, and I see the continuing frustration on the part of nonprofit staff members, their constituents, and their supporters. Individual donors represent 80% of all charitable giving, but many fundraisers are uncomfortable having an authentic relationship with these donors.

What's the answer?

Time and again, the answer, or at least the starting point to solving the problem, is to look at the donors. Why do donors give? How can nonprofits engage them in a way that will inspire them to give more? We know that most human beings have a desire to "give back." Couple that with the fact that more people are becoming wealthy, or wealthier, than ever before. This is especially true among groups often overlooked by the "traditional" fundraising targets, which have typically been older people who match the description of "givers" of the last century. If someone is a person of color, a woman, a young person, or any kind of donor who isn't the "usual suspect," chances are they won't have a place on most fundraisers' lists. If they haven't been a substantial donor to charities in the past, they might not even be able to get the attention of a nonprofit they're interested in knowing more about.

This has to change.

Since the 2020 publication of my first book, *Philanthropy Revolution: How to Inspire Donors, Build Relationships and Make a Difference* (HarperCollins), I've been, for thousands of fundraisers, the "de facto" voice of the major donor. For a very long time, the donor's actual voice hasn't been present in the conversation about how fundraisers can raise more money. More importantly, the conversation about how donors feel and why they donate has been notably absent. Why? Is it because fundraisers are intimidated by wealthy people? Maybe. I do know that (surprising to some) donors are intimidated by fundraisers! And just like any business or group that interacts with thousands, if not millions, of people, donors are living, breathing individuals who each do, hear, and say things differently than other people. Thinking of donors as a homogeneous group in which communication can be the same for everyone is a faulty strategy, but understanding donors as individuals can change that to a successful one. This book will give you quick and easy tools to help you see donors as the individuals they are and, in turn, teach you how to create an authentic, rewarding, and productive relationship with them.

The book's essays provide a roadmap for navigating twenty-first-century fundraising as it explores topics such as:

- The future of philanthropy: what does it look like and how can your team be the first to arrive?
- Demystifying the $234 billion opportunity of donor-advised funds
- The importance of adding millennials to your boards
- Why new tech tools cannot obscure meaningful donor relationships
- Avoiding tone-deaf outreach
- How to retain a recurring donor
- How not to lose a good fundraiser
- Types of giving: pledges, donations, planned giving, volunteering

The book concludes with a glossary that is designed to help both fundraisers and donors understand each other's vernacular. Having a conversation without understanding the terms used isn't helpful to anyone, and it can surely stop a potential donor relationship in its tracks.

Whether you work as a fundraiser, nonprofit leader, board member, volunteer, or anyone with a stake in the sustainability of a nonprofit organization, this book is for you. Here you will find the insight and tools you need to garner impactful support for the social and environmental causes we all care about. If you're ready to consider a change for the better, start reading!

THE ESSENTIAL
FUNDRAISER'S HANDBOOK

WHAT ALL FUNDRAISERS
NEED TO KNOW

CHAPTER 1

THE STATE OF PHILANTHROPY

Just the Facts, Ma'am

While speaking at the Association of Fundraising Professionals ICON 2023 conference, I presented some interesting statistics about a particular fundraising program for Dartmouth that had been a roaring success. What set this campaign apart from others was that it focused exclusively on women. Historically, Dartmouth's campaigns typically did well, and as of 2010, Dartmouth's capital campaign had raised significant revenue, including four donations of $1 million or more. In 2018, though, Dartmouth's fundraising became supercharged by including a new program that specifically targeted female alumni and widows of alumni. The result? From 2018 (when the women-focused campaign launched) to 2022, 144 women gave donations totaling $386 million, plus over $60 million in legacy giving pledges.

Surprised? According to a July 2020 McKinsey article entitled "Women as the Next Wave of Growth in US Wealth Management,"[1] "by 2030, American women are expected to control much of the $30 trillion in financial assets that baby boomers will possess—a potential wealth transfer of such magnitude that it approaches the annual GDP of the United States." Currently, 33% of millionaires in the US are women.[2] Research tells us that charitable giving overall, both in terms of donors and in terms of dollars, is continuing to decline. That research confirms that if we don't diversify our donor pool, the long-term sustainability of many nonprofit organizations (NPOs, also called NGOs) will be in jeopardy.

From the percentage of Americans who donate to charities to statistics on donor satisfaction and engagement, we will look at the state of philanthropy in the twenty-first century.

In this chapter, we'll cover:

- Percentage of households that give to charities over the years

- How the younger generation relates to giving
- How to keep donors interested and supporting your organization
- Protection from scandals

Numbers Don't Lie

Philanthropy is dying. It's unfortunate but true. And while not many people seem to want to talk about this impending doom in fundraising, the numbers undeniably support it. In 2001, 65% of households gave to charity. By 2015, this number had dropped to 56%.[3] From *The Chronicle of Philanthropy*:

> From 2000–2014, giving declined across every age group and every income and education level. Perhaps most frightening: the share of giving dropped most among 51- to 60-year-olds, who are often bedrock donors.[4]

And it goes deeper. Giving to religious institutions accounts for more than 30% of all giving, and givers who consider themselves religious tend to be among the most generous to all institutions, religious or not. But religious affiliation is way down in America (per the 2015 Pew report[5]), and along with it, religious giving. The share of Americans giving to religious causes has declined more than 10% in just the last few years.

When you look toward future generations of donors, the picture does not look any better. Our younger generations relate to causes differently and, therefore, give differently—they might install solar panels instead of giving to the Sierra Club. Or they might fund a friend directly in an online, crowd-sourced campaign. They definitely prefer startups to establishment behemoths, and they are eager to try different things, so their loyalties shift more frequently. While this is all characteristic of millennials, this way of thinking has proven attractive and contagious to Gen X and baby boomers as well.

Even the wealthiest Americans are giving a relatively insignificant amount when compared to their overall net worth. On his website, Inside Philanthropy, David Callahan, author of *The Givers*, writes:

Yes, affluent Americans have been giving more. But they've also been earning more, and it's far from clear that their giving has kept up with their new wealth accumulation. The top 1% has assets of $30 trillion, about a third of all household wealth. But these Americans gave away less than a half of 1% of their total wealth in 2016.

Not only are new gifts dropping across the board, but repeat donations are down even further, and charitable organizations have no idea how to turn things around. Because the turnover of fundraising professionals is so high, organizations want to get the most out of their development personnel as quickly as possible. This extremely short-sighted policy means that fundraisers are pushed to focus mostly on major gifts, which just contributes to the problem. It seems that every organization wants a development person to solve all their problems—and they want it now. When that fundraiser comes to an organization, the pressure is on to bring in big money immediately. Sadly, for most nonprofits, the idea of laying the groundwork for the future just isn't there.

In addition, the sheer number of nonprofits is increasing, when it seems pretty clear that many, if not most, should be merging and consolidating. The cost to keep an organization running (and pay a good development person the hefty salary they're worth) is increasing, and the boards of those organizations rarely want to "put themselves out of business" by merging with one or more other organizations. The board's reluctance to "wake up and smell the coffee" is a real problem, and so charity after charity does what they've always done— keep the status quo, ignore the disturbing trends, ask the "big guys" to increase their donation a bit more, and kick the can down the road.

I say let's expose these reticent, moribund organizations for what they are, and celebrate the ones that are taking the risk to change for the better.

Feelin' Groovy

For most nonprofits post-COVID, the question still remains about how best to interact with donors—and how to raise money to meet the budget in real time. It took a pandemic to teach us how to further deepen our relationships with donors and even get a little vulnerable. What we can take away from the pandemic is a lesson to remember during any future challenging times.

In my mind, a challenging time is a great time to continue, if not strengthen, your relationship with your donors. "Cultivate" and "steward" are words that are used often, and although I love the concept of "stewarding," that term feels impersonal and cold. Does anyone really want to be "stewarded"? It sounds a bit like being herded. No warm and fuzzy there. Better options might be "engaging," "interacting with," or even "listening to."

So what should a fundraiser/nonprofit professional be doing now to keep donors interested in supporting your organization? How can a development person recruit new donors when the "standard process" has been interrupted?

Let your donors in. Engage with your volunteers. Be genuine, authentic, and honest. When you do, everybody wins.

How can that be, you ask? If I'm not securing the donations I need to deliver, how do I win?

The answer lies in years of research into the benefits of volunteering and giving. Both volunteering *and* giving provide myriad emotional and psychological benefits to the volunteer[6] or donor and, simply said, they create happiness. Happier people—especially when their happiness was facilitated by your nonprofit—are more loyal, more concerned about the health of your organization, and, therefore, more likely to donate (and donate again).

Instead of thinking of fundraising as transactional, think of it as providing happiness. With nearly 41% of Americans surveyed reporting at least one adverse mental or behavioral health condition,[7] your donors and volunteers need you more than ever. For anyone who has been impacted by, or is connected to, your nonprofit or your cause, a non-transactional engagement with you is likely to create or enhance a long-term connection—and help these "fans" of your cause become happier.

So, how do you accomplish this? First, you have to let go of the transactional mindset. Yes, we know you need to raise that money, but for many people, you need to help them feel connected, heard, and cared for first.

Look further than your prospect list for fans of your cause. Pull together names and contact information of anyone and everyone who has been connected to, or strongly interested in, your organization and/or your cause. Not just donors! Then reach out to them to tell them—honestly—how your non-profit is dealing with the challenge at hand. Let them know about the hard choices you've had to make in order to protect the future of your organization. Let them know about the successes you've had—against all odds, at times—during these difficult months. Tell them about staff and constituents who have overcome challenges while staying committed to your cause.

Finally, ask for help! Whether it's via an online survey or focus groups, or just a special opportunity to engage with your organization's leaders (e.g., a Zoom webcast with a healthy amount of Q&A offered), engage these people with an eye toward creating a relationship that's more of a caring partnership than the usual donor/fundraiser paradigm.

As I've stated before, volunteers are a critical asset to your organization—extremely loyal, but often overlooked. Engage them, help them refocus their anxiety into feeling good about helping you do good, and everyone wins. How often do you get to do your job, support your mission, and also create happiness?

Scandals Are the New Norm

I woke up one morning thinking about one of the philanthropy scandals of the previous two months (I wish there was only one, but this is the one I was most upset about)—the Michael Steinhardt story. It's disturbing, still lacks true transparency, and it doesn't bode well for the future of giving.

Steinhardt[8] is one of the largest donors in the US today—witness his wings at the Met, hundreds of millions put into Birthright Israel, and his school at NYU. Steinhardt suggesting a fundraiser not come back asking for money until she has a husband and child, and saying that a young rabbi should be a donor's "concubine" is offensive enough, but it's even more creepy to learn that other leaders in Jewish philanthropy have suggested that this and other bad things might actually be okay—as long as they're offset by generous donations to charitable organizations. All I can say is "eeeeeew" and stress how wrong and disgusting that is.

Upon first reading the story, it's safe to say that some people might have thought, *Oh, well, this happy elder gentleman is probably just stuck in a past de-*

cade when this kind of talk was funny and he just isn't aware that times have changed. Unfortunately, that sentiment doesn't work when you see in the article that he was actually sued several years ago by two women in an art gallery because of his "harmless talk." He was clearly fully aware that times have changed. He just didn't care.

To their credit, many organizations immediately stepped up[9] and voiced their support for the brave women who spoke out against Steinhardt. But many remain mum to this day, two months later—which says a lot. It would be interesting to correlate the names of the organizations that responded (or didn't) with the amounts of money Steinhardt contributes to them.

As the chatter continues, at least one of the women who came forward was told, as recently as last week, that she should be "ashamed" for stepping forward and letting this information get "out." And Birthright has thousands of kids going to Israel this summer, happily accepting free trips courtesy, in part, of Steinhardt, who seems to have made it even more clear that nothing will make him happier than arranging a flurry of "hookups" (in the name of creating lots of Jewish babies, of course) while the young adults are partying in the desert. Go get 'em, boys!

There is some good happening to counteract and diffuse the actions of the Steinhardts of the world. I say "Awesome!" to the National Council of Jewish Women[10] who hired Steinhardt's victim and accuser Sheila Katz as their CEO within a week of the article's publication, and to the other dozens of women who have come forward with their own problematic Steinhardt stories. For those who haven't come forward because they're worried that they "won't work in this town again," I say, you no longer need to worry.

The bad guys, and/or the guys who "just talk that way," will keep doing what they're doing, and many charities will put aside their good judgment in order to get those charitable dollars. But word is out that this has to stop, and slowly, slowly, slowly, some of the charitable institutions in our country have not only taken notice, but they, like me and others I know, have become keenly aware of this issue—and if you're one of the many victims of this institutionally sanctioned sexual abuse, we're paying attention.

Watch out, nonprofits who look the other way when bad guys give you money. A new band of good guys (men and women) have your backs, and we're all about getting this information "out."

Remember that the "rules" from thirty or twenty or even ten years ago may be grossly outdated and even inappropriate today. If something you're told to say doesn't feel right, don't say it.

During any given day, we all do things a certain way. A great exercise is to ask WHY you do things that way. If the answer is "because we've always done it that way," think again. That's not a good answer.

In challenging times, connections are key. Let your donors in. Engage with your volunteers. Be genuine, authentic, and honest. And when you do, everybody wins.

Consider the emotional benefits of volunteering and giving. Instead of thinking of fundraising as transactional, think of it as providing happiness.

Money—lots of it—is being left on the table. The playbook that the charitable sector has been using is outdated, ineffective, and off-putting for many donors. Let's embrace change and create a new, better playbook.

CHAPTER 2

SOUND THE ALARM, IT'S TIME TO CHANGE

Data—Admit That You Don't Know Everything and Read the Research

Why do we continue to use a playbook from decades ago to guide our fundraising when it's not working so well? At a recent high-level fundraiser meeting, a fundraising professional reported customer retention rates for various business sectors. The customer retention rates in charitable giving were the lowest among all business sectors studied, and those rates were continuing to drop.

In order to reach new donors while continuing to best serve our existing base, it's time to look at the research; let the data motivate you to do better and get with the times!

In this chapter, we'll cover:

- Redirecting your resources away from Santa
- Reasons donors might only give in December
- Why non-December gift-giving is even more important
- How best to use your finely sharpened tools
- Changing how you accept donations
- Declining donor and retention rates

What's Wrong with May and June?

Ah, the beginning of a new year. The stress of December is behind us, and our inboxes (and junk-mail folders) are lighter than they've been in the last few months. Our snail mail has dramatically decreased, and those frantic fundraisers have all but disappeared.

As a donor, I'm continually surprised by the December onslaught of solicitations. I realize that one-third of all annual giving happens at the end of the calendar year, and so nonprofits gear up (just like retailers) to raise the most money possible during this time period. But why do the nonprofits think that I give—or want to give—my charitable gifts in December?

It seems that the December giving frenzy is self-perpetuating. The big pushes for gifts happen in December, so more money comes in December and, seeing that more money comes in at that time of year, NPOs direct more resources to December solicitations. It's kind of a vicious cycle, and it works for some people. For many of us, though, it doesn't work at all. In fact, it's as annoying as my dog Nugget eating my tennis shoes. I understand retailers throwing more resources at the holidays since many people buy their holiday gifts late in the year. But fundraising for nonprofits is different.

Do nonprofits need more money in December for some reason, other than for programs specific to the holidays? If I give an organization $500 on December 29 instead of January 10, will their programs run better? Is January money worth less than December money?

Of course not. In fact, because so many of us have gotten used to the December solicitations, we think that we must give in December. It's true that many nonprofits will solicit donors in December, even though they already gave in June or September. Monthly donors are also often pushed hard to give more in December because their recurring donation is considered a "different type of giving."

Why do I, and other donors, have to be pushed like crazy during December? Am I missing something? Here are some reasons why donors might do their giving (only) in December:

1. **December-related personas.** There is a great article from Bloomerang[1] that identifies donors who give in December as "Last Minute Leslie," "Reminder-Needed Robert," "Clockwork Carol," and "Waffling Walter." It's interesting to note that, with the exception of "Clockwork Carol," who might have a tried-and-true tradition of doing her charitable giving in December, all of the other personas could easily give at a different time of the year. Would they do so if the solicitations were at a different time of year?

2. **The "season of gratitude."** Everyone's shopping, giving holiday gifts, and celebrating (sort of). December's the season of gratitude—let's be grateful and give!

3. **Possible tax benefits.** The tax piece is always there and might be applicable to a given donor, but generally, it's a minor consideration. As any wealth manager will tell you, you don't give to a charity because of a tax deduction. That might be part of the reason, but it shouldn't be your driving motivation—even though you might get a tax deduction, it's rarely close to 100%, and it might even be insignificant. More importantly, any tax benefit is applicable all year long—the only reason to pay attention to it in December is that you didn't think of it earlier—or because you're being solicited at that time of year.

I hear that tax thing more often than any other reason for end-of-year giving.

However, I've scoured lots of why-do-folks-donate lists to see how important tax benefits are to giving decisions, and most of them don't even consider them part of the story. As UC Berkeley's Greater Good Science Center[2] tells us, there are loads of benefits to giving, and like many other top-reasons-to-give lists, taxes and the fact that it's December aren't included.

From a charitable organization's perspective, gifts given during the rest of the year are often even more important than the December gifts. Most nonprofits (again, like retailers) assume that most revenue will come at the end of the year, and they budget accordingly. But needs don't typically abide by a calendar, so many programs might have to wait for their funding until just after December, even though they desperately need the resources in the summer. (Once I learned that this was the case, I started doing my giving at "odd times" during the year—not December.)

From a donor's perspective, I like to think of the December holiday season as a time to enjoy friends and family, to relax, to work on projects I didn't get around to during the year, and to start creatively thinking about my goals and plans for the coming year. In addition, my kids are typically home from school and the household can be even more chaotic than usual. Finally, I spend loads of time in November and December giving thank-you gifts to vendors and professionals (and teachers!) who help us during the year. Because of the solicitation onslaught, any possibility of relaxing in December seems impossible, and those solicitations become annoying instead of compelling.

Here's an idea. Ask your donors if they're "Clockwork Carols" and if they just give in December because that's their tradition. If they do, great. If, like me, they would prefer to enjoy December without the solicitations and to be solicited instead at another time of year (in a respectful, authentic way, of course), follow their wishes. It might be that by doing so, you'll (a) not annoy them in December, (b) raise more money because you have time for a non-rushed discussion with them, and (c) help the cash flow become more consistent throughout the year.

For those donors using donor-advised funds (we'll demystify DAFs later), know that there's absolutely no reason for them to give in December, with the exception of those infrequent donors who simply prefer to donate then. For your other donors, just ask them when they do their giving. You might be surprised how many of them would be happy to give when your organization needs it most.

Donor Identity and the Toolshed

I have met two types of fundraisers in my career: those whose professional identities are rooted in relationships and those whose identities are rooted in their tools—what anthropologist Edward Hall referred to as extensions. In his book *Beyond Culture*, Hall explains how human beings have always counted on their extensions to externalize tasks and achieve greater levels of efficiency. Hall's caution is that extensions have a way of taking on a life of their own, eventually leaving us feeling helpless without them and panicked when they stop doing their jobs as effectively as we expect.

Shortly after our planet came to a screeching halt in March 2020, I watched as one of our colleagues described the experience of having one's identity deeply rooted in an extension. In a vulnerable YouTube video, he described himself as having lost his superpower. Special events, his "superpower" and career-long extension of choice, were suddenly ill-suited for a world now navigating its way through a global pandemic. He explained that his passion had always been to help nonprofits raise money via special events. He described himself as perhaps one of the best in the country at his craft. Now, coming to grips with the scary realization that his particular skill no longer worked as well as it was supposed to, he was forced to confront the fact that our extensions have a tendency to let us down.

This is what most concerns me about an entire cohort of today's fundraisers—their professional identities have become tightly intertwined with a particular tool rather than the relationships these tools were intended to help them cultivate. Instead of becoming professionals known for cultivating superior relationships with our donors, this cohort is content to raise our expectations of the tools that can do the job for us.

History has taught us what holding too tightly to an extension looks like. In 1949, the Mann Gulch fire in Montana's Helena National Forest took the lives of thirteen firefighters. Over time, researchers were able to make sense of what had gone wrong: their leader had given them instructions that were at odds with their professional identities. To their surprise, the improvising leader told them to drop their tools and, instead of trying to outrun the fire, quickly clear an area where they could lie down and allow the fire to move over them. These instructions were more than confusing; they were antithetical to everything the firefighters knew about their roles, and they immediately created panic and an existential crisis much like our colleague experienced in the spring of 2020.

Unable to make sense of their rapidly changing environment, the firefighters in Mann Gulch maintained their tight grip on their tools and continued trying to outpace the fire instead of listening to their leader's directions, which could have saved them. When rescuers found these men's bodies, their hands were still tightly gripping their tools.

It's important we remember that our extensions aren't necessarily tangible tools we can hold in our hands; they can also be the mental models we construct. For example, the notion of an annual fund or a capital campaign is an extension that puts what is otherwise a complex and messy process into a neat, tidy box. So many of my colleagues have become master technicians at direct response, major gifts, and grant writing and have proven themselves remarkably capable of achieving their goals in the stable environments for which these tools were designed. Unfortunately, what very few of us were told early in our careers is that any extension is inclined to let us down in unforeseeable ways when the world becomes messy and unpredictable.

In a rapidly changing world, the fundraiser whose identity is wrapped up in holding on too tightly to a particular tool is also the fundraiser who will find themselves in the midst of an identity crisis when the unexpected happens. Hall wanted us to understand the risks of transferring higher levels of responsibility to our extensions, thereby diminishing our ability to do things ourselves. He also wanted us to make sense of the fact that when we rely on an extension, we give up some measure of context that we would expect to be there if we were to do the job ourselves. For example, sending a letter or email affords efficient communication; however, we miss out on the eye contact and body language that enhances communication when we're seated at a table with someone.

What the sector needed most in the midst of the recent pandemic was not masters of their extensions; we needed fundraisers who knew how to put down their tools, initiate genuine conversations, listen, and discern whether the timing of a request was right or wrong. When I think back on the number of success stories I have heard about fundraisers effectively navigating the pandemic, the common denominator has been the ability to let go of an extension or abandon some kind of tool or convention to discover where their real superpower resides.

Old-School or Archaic?

"Old-school" (per Merriam-Webster) definition:[3] "adhering to traditional policies or practices; characteristic or evocative of an earlier or original style, manner, or form."

"Archaic" (per Vocabulary.com) definition:[4] "something that belongs to an earlier or antiquated time. It can also mean something that is outdated but can still be found in the present and therefore could seem out of place."

There are still many folks in fundraising (and other sectors) who are so intimidated by technology that they rely on the good ol' checkbook because it's as comfortable and familiar as, well, tuna casserole. I'm happy that fundraising professionals are comfortable, but that doesn't mean the donors you're soliciting are.

In some areas, old-school can be cool and compelling. Archaic, on the other hand, is almost always the opposite of compelling. In fundraising, neither old-school nor archaic actions or policies are likely to result in a donation.

Looking at the way we accept donations, neither the old-school nor the archaic serves us well. It's time to "get with the times." To that end, let's examine some stats that will hopefully help you recognize the imperative to change how you accept donations:

- **Checks**

  Per 2016-2020 studies by the Federal Reserve on consumer payment choice,[5] the edict "Come back from the meeting with a check!" is not so applicable anymore. According to their findings, cash payments dropped from 31% in 2016 to 26% in 2019, payments using credit cards rose from 18% to 24%, debit card payments increased from 27% to 30%, and electronic payments squeezed up another point from 10% to 11%. Checks, however, managed to fall below their already low usage of 7% in 2016 to 5% in 2019.

- **Donor-advised funds**

  With approximately $234 billion sitting in donor-advised funds (DAF accounts), most nonprofits still make a DAF donor jump through hoops to give via this method. This is easily remedied by clearly stating on all of your solicitations that "DAF donations are welcomed" and giving the organization's mailing address and tax ID number. (Important note: if you're offering an incentive to give, promoting a matching gift program, or selling tickets/sponsorships for an event, make sure the DAF method of giving is as seamless as the other types of payment you're promoting.)

- **Forms of payment**

  I love the way the tool "Fundraise Up"[8] treats payment acceptance language on their website—"All Popular Payment Methods Accepted." They forgot a few (e.g., Venmo, Zelle, and others) but it's worth learning from this good example.

- **Recurring donations**

  Some fundraisers have been hesitant to accept recurring donations (where a credit card is kept on file and automatically charged monthly) because they don't want to deal with the issue of the card being expired, lost, or otherwise no longer valid. This decision is clearly leaving a great deal of money on the table, as 89% of millennials, 78% of Gen X, and 67% of boomers are enrolled in subscription services, and approximately 35% of the total US population is enrolled in some type of autopay program. The "expired card" issue is easily remedied via simple email notifications that are sent to the user with a kind note asking for new card information (with a simple button on the email that allows the user to fill in the information immediately.) An article from *NonProfit Pro*[7] gives some great advice on solving this problem: "Use everything in your power to get that update as soon as possible, so there's no lapse in payment."

It seems obvious to most, but if you don't know what Square and Swipe and Venmo are, please learn. These are as standard and ubiquitous today as checkbooks were in decades past. Keep the checks as a form of payment, but add just about anything a donor might want to pay with. After all the hard work that fundraisers do, it would be a shame to lose a gift because of the payment method.

Ignore Donor Retention Rates at Your Peril

I was at a conference recently where a participant reported customer retention rates for various business sectors. I knew that the nonprofit sector's retention rates were low and decreasing, but I was surprised at the difference between nonprofits and other sectors relative to customer retention. Here's a snapshot of those statistics:

- The average customer retention rate across all industries is about 75.5%.
- The media and the professional services industries both have the highest worldwide customer retention rate at 84% each.
- The hospitality, travel, and restaurant industries have the lowest customer retention rate at 55%, followed by retail at 63%.

In comparison, the nonprofit sector's average retention rates hover between 40% and 45%. I'm not sure about you, but I find that astonishing and depressing. When you add the following statistics to the mix and throw in a recession and/or economic instability, you have what some might call a crisis.

- The percentage of donors who gave in 2021 and then gave again in 2022 **decreased by 6.2% year over year** (per the FEP 2022 First Quarter Fundraising Report). Despite some saying that this was due to COVID giving being unusually high in 2020 and 2021, it's important to note that the percentage of donors who gave in 2019 (before COVID) and then again in 2020 dropped by 4.1% (per an FEP 2021 report). Sounds like a trend to me.
- The percentage of donors who give to a specific organization only once (ever) is nearly 70%. **Seven out of ten newly acquired donors**—likely highly solicited, and therefore highly costly—**won't be giving to that organization again** ever.
- The percentage of donors who give once and give again to the same organization the following year has been in the 18–20% range for many years now.
- Also, according to the FEP, **the recapture rate for lapsed donors is 4%.** At the same time, I've seen articles online (by reputable businesses) saying that regaining lapsed donors is more cost-effective than acquiring new ones. Really?

As a fundraiser, do you ever feel like you're spinning or on a treadmill? (Yes, I know the answer for most of you.) With the statistics listed above, it's no wonder. You have to work on recruiting new donors while knowing that more than half of them won't give again.

Maybe it's time to do things differently. Maybe it's time to look at a larger potential donor population, no? If we embrace change—immediate change—we can alter the trajectory of the donor churn rate. If, instead, we continue to work the same way because "that's the way we do it," then we can expect to stay on that treadmill.

Top Tips for Change

Ignore younger donors at your peril. You need them, and you need them now.

If you're thinking about solutions to challenges and you find yourself saying, "But we tried that already!" examine that carefully. Chances are you've tried those solutions in a different way or at a different time or with different people. Looking at solutions today, with your current staff, might be just like trying anew, and it just might work now when it didn't before.

Look at your annual fundraising calendar. Think about each event as if it could take place at any date during the year. If it *must* be in the third week of March, for example, ask why. If your answer is "Because it's always been at that time," think again.

Know the new payment options. Square, Swipe, Venmo . . . these are as standard and ubiquitous today as checkbooks were in decades past.

Your real superpower is in creating and nurturing relationships, not grasping tightly to your tools. In a rapidly changing world, the fundraiser whose identity is wrapped up in holding on too tightly to a particular tool is also the fundraiser who will find themselves in the midst of an identity crisis when the unexpected happens.

CHAPTER 3

AUTHENTICITY

Trust: It's Everything

I previously gave to a nonprofit organization that I had been introduced to by a colleague and friend. I think the NPO is wonderful; I love their work. Once that organization recognized me as a larger donor, I was invited to private events which were led by the organization's regional director. Unfortunately, this regional director exhibited neither warmth nor authenticity when we met, and had zero apparent desire for any kind of relationship. (It felt a bit like being in a room with the "mean girl" in high school.)

After attending other events with that organization where I got the same impression, I stopped giving. I tried to rationalize this decision (why should the organization suffer because of a single staff member?) but I just couldn't get past it. I could actually feel the tenacity of that first impression continuing to hamper any efforts they made to create a relationship with me (which were almost nonexistent anyway). Missed opportunity on their part, right?

Let's look at how today's successful nonprofits create and sustain authentic, trusting, and long-term relationships with donors.

In this chapter, we'll cover:

- Losing prospective donors due to lack of "romance"
- Public recognition: is your donor approach condescending?
- The wrong way to send direct mail
- The right way to send direct mail
- Seven ways to make a great first impression

Relentless

Sometimes, I felt like I was the only one out there being hit with a bunch of crazy—and often offensive—solicitations. And then I found the 2020 Alumni Access® VAESE Alumni Benchmarking Study.[1]

Although this study mainly addresses colleges and universities, the statistics generated are applicable to almost any nonprofit organization. Here are some highlights from the report:

- In all responding institutions, the average number of gift solicitations sent to first-year graduates has increased from 3.7 to 3.9 solicitations per institution per year since 2017.
- The number of schools that send five or more gift solicitations to new graduates during their first year is up 55% from 2015.
- 46% of participating institutions report soliciting first-year graduates ten or more times during that first year after graduation.
- 15% of these institutions send twenty or more solicitations to new grads during the first year.

As the report's editor, Gary Toyn, writes:

> If the best practice is to "romance" (cultivate) alumni long before you make a "request" (ask for money), why are **78% of higher education institutions soliciting their first-year graduates?** Especially considering how many of these new graduates are just launching their professional career, and have barely moved out of the dorms or their parents' basement. And that says nothing about soliciting graduates who have an average student loan balance of $35,359.

Who decided that this makes sense? If we asked the staff in those university advancement departments how they (personally) would feel if they received ten or more solicitations from the same organization in a given year, what would they say? My guess is that most of them would be annoyed. For some, that warm, fuzzy feeling about the institution they just graduated from (alma mater literally meaning "nourishing mother") will disappear, and they might want nothing to do with said alma mater ever again.

The new VAESE study reveals a trend toward a greater number of alumni "opting out" of contact with their alma mater:

- Since 2015, alumni organizations have experienced a 15% increase in the number of alumni who have asked to be put on the "do-not-contact" or "do-not-solicit" list (referred to as "opting out" of contact with their alma mater).
- In 46% of alumni organizations, at least 10% of their alumni have permanently opted out.
- The number of institutions with at least a 10% opt-out rate has increased 79% since 2015.

Think there's a correlation here between the persistent asking and the opt-out rate? Even though there might be other forces at work (the report also finds that over 80% of alumni professionals surveyed say their alumni see little or no value in the benefits provided), it seems extremely likely and logical that the incessant solicitations are a big part of the story.

I know that some fundraisers will say that the 80/20 rule[2] keeps their organizations running, but what about all those twenty-somethings who will be completely turned off by your organization because of your heavy-handedness? One of the promises of higher education is that graduates will be set on a path to be successful in their careers. The promise isn't that they'll be successful in the first year after graduating—it's more that the trajectory after graduating will result in success via higher earning potential.

If that's the case, then why are many of those same institutions willing to lose the relationship with an increasing number of their alumni before they even get started in their careers?

When my son graduated from university several years ago, I returned home after the commencement ceremony to find a solicitation addressed to him—asking for a donation. Can you say "mood-killer"?

No Harm, No Foul? For Donor Recognition, Think Again.

I have a friend who went to an event recently where there was a walk-through of a fairly large donor-funded facility that was still under construction. The site was well-designed, and a staff member enthusiastically gave a tour, explaining which functions would be done in each area. The presentation was for a small group of major donors.

All seemed terrific until the development person in tow spoke. There was no "Thanks for coming" or "Isn't this exciting." Instead, the only time she spoke was when she pointed to a smallish wall and said, ". . . and here's the donor recognition area!" The room got very quiet and everyone kept walking. In the next area, again the development person pointed to yet another wall and said ". . . and here's where the donor names will go!" (In case you're wondering—yes, these statements were made with a big smile and lots of excitement/enthusiasm. Not so much enthusiasm was returned by the donors in the room.)

When I hear this story—and many others like it—I can't help but get queasy. It would be one thing to show the location of the "donor recognition wall" if one of the donors asked about it, but without context (other than that there was a room of donors), the comments were, at best, off-putting, tacky, and, in my opinion, inappropriate. Why would someone assume that the location of a donor recognition wall would make a difference in the size of gift someone was considering? What drives me most crazy about this story is that the development person just assumed that the donors in the room cared about public recognition.

Donors come in all shapes and sizes, and most generalizations about donors, if not all, won't apply to many of them. Donors, like anyone else, are human beings with their own hopes, dreams, feelings—and reasons for giving. To suggest that anyone with financial resources who chooses to give to nonprofits does so because they want their "name in lights" is just plain condescending. Maybe even just lazy. Assuming that "all donors _____" (fill in the blank) suggests there isn't time or an inclination to speak to donors as individuals. Having those individual conversations about public recognition will clearly tell a fundraiser where the donor is on the donor recognition spectrum.

Imagine a donor recognition continuum where one end is *anonymous* and the other end is *name in lights with a marching band*. Somewhere between those two is where most donors are (in terms of how they want to be recognized). In a healthy, sustainable donor/fundraiser relationship, it's easy for the two parties to discuss how the donor feels about recognition.

In fact, in a recent study from Vanderbilt University about donor behavior relative to public recognition, the researchers (both professors at prestigious universities) discovered that "nonprofit organizations often use various forms of public-facing recognition, from giving walls to galas, to acknowledge donations and encourage giving. New research suggests tactics like these may actually discourage the likelihood of donation."[3] It's worth reading.

In another study published in *Blue Avocado*, "Still Publishing Donor Names? Ditch the List,"[4] researchers looked—in great detail—at the published donor list, which just might be one of those things that we do mostly because "that's what we've always done." Turns out that the time and money your organization spends on those lists might not be helpful, in terms of bringing in more revenue, at all.

The bottom line is, as always, to stop assuming. The best way to fully understand a donor's wishes relative to public recognition? Just ask them. Note that "public recognition" is different from saying thank you. Everyone deserves a thank you.

My Fraught Relationship with Direct Mail

As you might imagine, I receive a large number of direct mail solicitations from charitable organizations. Many of them get tossed in the trash without being opened, but occasionally, something about them makes me take a closer look. I spend a lot of time helping fundraisers understand how a (major) donor feels about their fundraising methods, so let me tell you how a donor (this donor) feels about direct mail specifically.

I keep hearing about direct mail being an effective piece of the charitable fundraising arsenal—that the open rate is far higher than email, the response rate is far higher than email, and that people really enjoy seeing direct mail solicitations in their mailbox. Personally, that seems strange to me, but as many fundraising professionals have told me, "You're not the target audience for this." Okay, but I still keep getting direct mail over and over and over again—so someone out there thinks that I'm the target audience for their solicitations. Or, more likely, the sending organization doesn't care that I'll likely just toss what I get since I'm not their target audience anyway. Maybe worst of all, when faced with the seemingly daunting task of segmenting their mailing list, they just throw up their hands and send their mailing out to their entire database.

I know that many of you spend lots of time making sure that targeted donors are receiving the solicitation appropriate for them, but especially with larger nonprofits, I don't see it. Recently, I received a number of annoying direct mail solicitations. How annoying? Annoying enough that I will likely never forget the solicitation, and my annoyance will be forever attached to that nonprofit.

I received a solicitation about a year ago from a large organization that I had actually hosted a major fundraising event for in the past. I only agreed to host the event because I believed in the organization—their senior staff, their mission, and their history of success. Now I hear the name of that NPO and I can't help but cringe, because just hearing their name reminds me that they sent me a snail mail solicitation telling me that my payment was past due. Was that printed like an old-fashioned "past due" stamp—in red ink and on an angle on the envelope? Yes, it was.

Was I curious about what was inside—and compelled to open the envelope? Yes. Was I furious when I saw that they had asked me to give them a larger donation this year, with strange numbers showing on the enclosed "remittance form"—in little boxes that I was asked to check? Affirmative. Note that other than supporting this NPO by hosting an event at my home, I had never sent a donation to this organization. Not once.

Some direct mail marketers say that one of the many benefits of direct mail is that it's memorable. Yup—this was memorable, but not in the way that I think they wanted.

That was a long time ago, but just in the last twenty-four hours, I received two different direct mail pieces—each from a large, respected institution—that I found irritating (I'm being nice with that word). I put them both on my desk so that I could look at them hours later to see if maybe I wouldn't be so upset upon a subsequent reading.

That didn't happen. In fact, I can feel my heart rate increasing again just looking at them while I'm writing this. The mailers shared something in common. They both thanked me for my "ongoing support" of their nonprofit. That's lovely, but I hadn't made any contribution to those organizations last year. Or the year before. Or ever. Yes, it was my name and address on the mailer.

To give me that "personal feeling," I suppose, the letters expressed thanks for my "courage" and stated that I was an "inspiration" and a "steadfast supporter." They also thanked me for my "annual contribution" (annual? really?), and one of them listed my "Gift Summary" for the previous year. (Yes, it was blank.)

I'm certain that:

1. I'm not the only person, nor the only "major" donor, getting solicitations like this.
2. Direct mail works for some organizations, but probably (hopefully?) not with letters worded the way mine were.
3. This can be done better, and we likely don't need to "throw the baby out with the bathwater" because different people have different preferences relative to communication.
4. If these organizations had cared a bit more about the recipient, they wouldn't have thanked me for something I hadn't done.

When they sent these mailings, I had a moment of confusion. How is it possible that a major, highly respected institution could send out a solicitation like this? The tone and contents of the letter (and remittance form) seemed diametrically opposed to the brand logo I was looking at. As any brand marketer can tell you, this is not the result any organization is looking for. In case you're wondering, I do appreciate some direct mail. My favorite example is one I wrote about in a *Philanthropy 451* post:

A better idea might be something like the postcard I received recently from a political candidate I supported, thanking me for a donation by succinctly telling me what my donation allowed her to achieve. It was simple, clear, had a great photo on one side, and made me feel glad to know my gift meant something.

That is a direct mail piece that I will remember, and you better believe that if and when that person asks for a donation again, I will happily contribute.

The recent "Trust in Civil Society"[5] reports by Independent Sector (well worth reading) tell us that about 56% of Americans trust nonprofits—almost the same percentage in 2022 as in 2021. That still leaves a whole lot of people who don't trust nonprofits, or who don't care either way. It also says that Gen Z is "skeptical of the sector" and many prefer giving to individuals rather than a large organization. The report also says that "public trust is the currency of the nonprofit sector." That makes sense, right?

Sometimes It's the Little Things

I returned from a lengthy road trip with my teenage daughter; it had been an eye-opener in numerous ways. We visited a dozen different cities and nearly as many states—most of which I'd never been to. About halfway through the trip, I realized that I had been judging the cities based on brief interactions I'd had with the people I'd met in the hotels we'd stayed in. I got my initial feeling about a city based on those first impressions.

I recognize this might not be a fair way to assess a place, but as human beings, we react based on the input that comes our way. As per this Kellogg/Trust Project report,[6] the study's findings tell us that trustworthiness is something people judge automatically, even before we've gotten our wits together to determine how confident we are in our judgment.

The same Kellogg report went even further by applying these findings to determining how trust influences giving (in this case, in the context of investing with a trustee). The upshot of this team's multi-year research was that we essentially judge people on two dimensions:

1. How warm is this person? (So, how benevolent is this person?)
2. How competent is this person? (Does this person have the capability of acting on his or her intentions?)

In the case of my trip, I was judging the city by what I encountered in these tiny moments of time. More important than the hotel facility itself, my first impressions were set by my interactions (or desire for interactions) with the hotel staff. Applying this to nonprofit fundraising, I now see that, as a donor, many of my decisions about giving to an organization (or not) are a result of my first interaction with a fundraiser.

At the beginning of this chapter, I mentioned my experience meeting the regional director of an NPO I liked and quickly feeling like I was in a room with the mean girl in high school. In real-life fundraising interactions, whether they're online or offline, that first impression you make with a prospective donor has a high probability of impacting your ability to secure a gift from them.

1. Don't pander—doing so is sure to create a negative impression.
2. Don't assume. Instead, ask!
3. Be authentic—donors are usually interested in relationships, not transactions.
4. Think about who the donor is as an individual.
5. Think about how the donor feels (base it on how you would feel in that situation).
6. Be honest (donors can see through a "tap dance").
7. Share your enthusiasm and dedication to your organization's mission.

Remember that the impression you give when interacting with someone determines trustworthiness. Trust, in turn, determines giving—not only for now but in the long term. Family wealth expert Dennis Jaffe writes about the positive effect on a relationship when trust is intact, including improved communication about the relationship and how it's working. He also points out the detrimental effect on a relationship when trust is lost. In "The Essential Importance Of Trust: How To Build It Or Restore It," published in *Forbes*[7] in 2018:

> If the level of trust is low in a relationship or organization, people limit their involvement and what they are willing to do or share . . . But, more often than not, people feel that their distrust is not safe to share. So a leader or loved one may be slow to discover that they have lost a person's

trust ... How can you fix something that is not expressed or shared? How do you even know that trust is lost?

One way is for the relationship to begin with a positive first impression. If those first milliseconds when you meet someone are engaging (in a good way), then that initial impression can serve to protect the relationship going forward. If trust is established on day one, then a donor, for example, is more likely to let you know if they have an issue. It might feel like a little thing, but that initial "meeting" has big ramifications.

Top Tips for Trust and Authenticity

Please stop the practice of sending direct mail solicitations saying "It's time to renew" to people who've never given to you. If this is your strategy, it won't work.

If you want to keep a new donor, don't assume their gift is annual. Don't assume that if they give, the dollar amount will increase each time they donate. Most donors don't know that "rule," and many will stop giving if you make it clear that you're not satisfied with the same size gift as last year.

Don't tell a donor you're not going to ask for money and then ask for money. Nothing ruins trust faster.

Does starting an email with "Today is Your Last Chance" really bring in funds? It sounds morbid to me. (And of course, it's not true . . .) Maybe it's better to say something like "Our budget will be finalized today. Your gift today will allow us to increase the number of people we're helping in the coming year."

If a donor just isn't into what you're "selling," let it go. Better yet, use their interests to refer them to someone whose nonprofit is a better match for them in terms of mission. Doing so is the difference between a relationship and a transaction.

WHAT YOU CAN DO
TO START RAISING MONEY RIGHT NOW

CHAPTER 4

DONOR RELATIONSHIPS

Your Assumptions Are Holding You Back from Success

I often receive emails and texts asking me for advice. Typically, the questions are about fundraising—specifically, how to secure a donation from someone like me. That's great and I enjoy providing the advice.

Occasionally, though, the sender wants to ask me "generic" or theoretical questions about obtaining a gift in general, but after some quick back-and-forth messaging, they ask me point-blank to personally fund their organization. I don't love that part. (Especially because, by doing so, it's clear they haven't read my writings.) No relationship in this scenario.

So, let's answer the most-asked question, look at some erroneous assumptions, widen the lens on where to find financial support, keep you from making the mistake the sender above made, and talk about one of the most important relationships your nonprofit will ever have: the one with your donors.

In this chapter, we'll look at:

- Why would a donor want to support your nonprofit?
- What are your donors all about?
- Four questions to ask your donors
- How assumptions are hindering your organization
- Eight assumptions you should make about donors
- Key details to have in place for your donors

The Short Answer to the Most-Asked Question

A reader asked me an interesting question. She asked what I, personally and as a donor, need to experience from a nonprofit in order to want to support them financially.

Good question. As many of you know, I provide answers to that in *Philanthropy Revolution* and in the many podcasts and lectures I've participated in.

However, the fundraiser was asking for a quick-and-dirty shortlist of tips to use immediately.

I can do the shortlist, as long as you, the reader, realize it's not a comprehensive answer. If "short and simple" got donors to give money to nonprofits, nobody would need the myriad of books and other publications out there that provide professional advice to fundraisers and nonprofit leaders. But I understand that sometimes, to get started on a new path, you need to keep it simple.

Here's my short answer to the question, and although these tips won't necessarily get you a donation, they'll at least get you started on the path to doing so. The first hurdle is realizing that change is necessary and, in this case, a very good thing. Once you accept that, try this:

1. Treat the donor as you would want to be treated. Don't pander and don't assume.

2. Convey to the donor why you're doing the hard work of fundraising and why you (personally) have dedicated your time to what your organization does. Be clear on what your group's mission is.

3. If the potential donor isn't "into" what your NPO does, let it go. Better yet, if you know another organization that does fit the interests of that potential donor, make the connection to them!

4. Be clear to the donor about one or more particular needs you have. The more specific, the better (e.g., "We could help five more kids if we had more funds . . ." or "We recognize a need for this particular project, but we can't do it without an infusion of resources").

5. If possible, give the potential donor an opportunity to give something non-monetary to the organization. If they want to "get their hands dirty," tell them about the volunteer opportunities you have. There is no reason to keep volunteers siloed from donors. (In fact, doing so couldn't be more counterproductive in the big picture.)

6. Most importantly, see if you can build an authentic relationship with the donor based on your shared passion for the cause. If you have that, asking for funding isn't so challenging—in fact, they might even ask YOU how they can make the most impact.

Remember that donors are human beings, and all of us—regardless of our means—have donated something to someone at some time. Once you accept that fact, it's easier to see how a donor might respond to your pitches. If you (personally) would be turned off by your pitch, chances are good that the donor you're soliciting will feel the same way.

Simple Ways to Learn About Your Donors

I love it when I'm asked: "How do I know what my donors are all about?" I love it because the answer—at least the first, high-level answer—is so simple. The answer is: "Just ask them."

When I suggest that answer, I often get a confused stare, and sometimes I watch the fundraiser break out in a cold sweat. Why does this happen? It happens because some fundraisers believe that donors are alien creatures who are unapproachable, cranky, condescending, and generally unpleasant to be around.

The truth, of course, is that some donors are those things, but the vast majority are ordinary people who are approachable, kind, and giving for the right reasons. When soliciting donors, we're dealing with a subset of the population, and by looking at our database, we already know a few things about them:

1. We know where they live, what they do (or did) for a living, and maybe a bit about their family members.
2. We might know "where the money came from"—although not always.
3. We know that, according to our research or personal knowledge, tey have the resources to make a substantive gift to our nonprofit.
4. Depending on the research we have, we might know their political party, religion, and maybe what boards they're on.

That's a great start. But here's the rub. None of those pieces of information tell us anything about them as individual human beings. None of that tells us much, if anything, about their hopes and dreams and what they care about. For fundraisers looking to build a relationship (and I hope all of you are!), there's not much in this "data" that helps us when we're about to have a one-on-one conversation with a prospect.

There are two things you can and should do right now—before you enter into a conversation with someone you might find a bit intimidating. First, do what I call a "Five-Minute Google Search." You should be doing this for all of your prospects to learn more about them as people. This is not about corroborating your data—it's about getting a sense of what they're about as human beings.

The second, in my opinion, is the most important. **Ask them these four questions.** (The method of asking doesn't matter so much—but I recommend an online survey like Survey Monkey, which should take you less than an hour to create. And the cost is minimal, if anything.)

1. **How do you like to be addressed?** (This usually refers to name tags or a mailing—something written.) Everyone knows what makes them the most comfortable—the traditional "formal" approach, a more casual approach, Mr. or Mrs. or Doctor or Professor (or none of the above). Just ask them and they will tell you.

2. **How do you prefer to be communicated with?** This is pretty straight-forward—and has been used in most doctor's offices for years—but for some reason is rarely asked in nonprofits' communication. Answers are simple and multiple-choice: phone (with a subcategory of mobile or landline), text, email, snail mail, etc. Give them an "any of the above" option too.

3. **How often would you like to know about our impact?** Choices are also multiple, including "annually," "quarterly," "monthly," or "as good things happen."

4. **How do you like to be thanked?** This one is rarely asked of donors— and fundraisers often just assume that a donor would appreciate a thank you in a certain way. The truth is that donors differ greatly in how they want to be thanked. If you get it wrong, you're likely to turn the donor off completely. Permanently. Instead of guessing, just ask! Note that the continuum of choices can run the gamut from "keep it anonymous" to "send a marching band with banners in my name."

Most will fall somewhere in between those, and this is also the place where you can find out who loves a handwritten thank-you note, who prefers a phone call, and who is just fine with an email thank you—as long as it comes quickly after the donation is made. In this category, it's also important to note that many people aren't comfortable saying what they want out loud, so you're much more likely to get an honest answer when they're filling out the survey.

You can add whatever additional questions you like, but keep it short and simple. The best thing about these surveys is that they provide an invisible, but extremely important, benefit. They "telegraph" to the donor that you see them as an individual and that you will act on their survey preferences as they have communicated. (Do not ask them any of these questions if you aren't prepared to follow through on doing what they've asked.)

One of my clients told me that after sending out one of these surveys, he got notes to the effect of "thanks for asking—I didn't know you cared." Really.

Do these surveys on a regular schedule to reinforce the "I-see-you-as-an-individual" message. And once you convey that message, your donors will be much more open and comfortable with you, and you will be much more comfortable talking with them about their hopes and dreams.

Empathy, a Pandemic, and Donors

I'm not sure if it's a post-pandemic realization or if people are finally catching on that change is necessary, but I'm feeling lots of new energy in the research space—especially where it involves people and emotions. Research on things like empathy, connection, engagement, decision-making, and communication seems to be the focus of a number of studies that have taken place since COVID entered the picture.

Is this a natural result of two years of confusion and fear? The research shows that, since spring of 2020, at least 50% of our population has experienced an increase in stress and anxiety, 54% are emotionally exhausted, 53% describe themselves as "sad," and 50% are irritable (*Forbes*[1] and Qualtrics[2]). It sure seems like COVID was a clear contributor, if not *the* contributor, to those numbers.

Another study[3] from Medicare in August 2020 found that one in four American adults aged 65 and older had reported symptoms of anxiety or depressive disorder, compared with a study in 2018 that showed the same symptoms occurring in one in ten older American adults.

It's clear that people are stressed, anxious, and/or depressed in a way that hasn't been seen in a very long time. This is where the new focus on empathy comes in. Knowing that people are having a hard time mentally, emotionally, and financially, those in the business of engaging individuals have to adjust their methods of interaction. In fact, it's critical, whichever sector you find yourself in (business, education, nonprofits, etc.), to realize that your success rate will be largely determined by the way you empathize with the person with whom you're interacting.

A lot of similar studies were done in the for-profit sector, but I wondered what it would look like to take some of this fascinating and important research and apply it to nonprofits. Check it out—it's pretty clear by looking at these studies that changing the word "leaders" to "nonprofit" and "employees/people" to "donors" gives us a clear message about working with donors in a post-pandemic climate. (The information below is from a recent Catalyst[4] study detailed in *Forbes*.)

1. "Engagement. 76% of people who experienced empathy from their leaders reported they were engaged compared with only 32% who experienced less empathy."

    Translated into nonprofit-world terms, we can read this as donors experiencing empathy from fundraisers are 34% more likely to be engaged than donors facing a fundraiser (or fundraising message) that lacks empathy. If you're a fundraiser or nonprofit leader, it looks like you'll have more than double the engagement rate (and, it follows, success raising money) if you show empathy to your prospects. Let's make that *authentic* empathy while we're on the subject . . .

2. "Retention. 57% of white women and 62% of women of color said they were unlikely to think of leaving their companies when they felt their life circumstances were respected and valued by their companies."

The article added that those numbers dropped to 14% and 30% respectively when value and respect were absent. Let's read that as—female donors are about twice as likely to continue engaging with fundraisers if they feel that their personal life experiences are respected. With the retention of donors being top of the list for most nonprofit organizations, these statistics are dramatic. Respecting someone's "life circumstances" when you're engaging with them makes a huge difference in their "stickiness"—likelihood to continue giving to you. (In case you're thinking that this sounds like the definition of a relationship, you're correct.)

If I as a donor feel that the person asking me for a gift is empathetic—caring about me as a person and not a piggy bank—we might both become more empathetic. Empathy fosters more empathy. How great is it to connect with a donor via an empathetic, authentic, and likely long-term relationship? Isn't giving about having empathy for a situation or cause? I love this quote from the Greenstein Family Foundation:[5] "Giving is in a tug-of-war between strategy and empathy, but the best kind of philanthropy is one that incorporates both."

Looking at this from a nonprofit and donor perspective, I can read this as strong support for fundraisers to show that they authentically care about donors as people. Of course, that also means the fundraiser needs to actually listen to the donor and adjust to their (in this case, emotional) needs.

For the fundraiser, this can make their job much more meaningful and fulfilling. For both the donor and the fundraiser, getting past the archaic "scripted" interactions and into the realm of an actual relationship is likely to foster compassion, action, and long-term giving.

Let's take the well-being of your nonprofit one step further to include empathy and compassion. The research is in. And now, post-pandemic, we can learn from the information recent studies share about empathy, connection, and engagement making a difference between your donors—and fundraisers—feeling they are merely part of a transaction or a valued part of a relationship.

*Making an A** Out of You and Me*

Most people know that making assumptions—about anyone or anything—is often a mistake. In fact, I did a quick search on Google and found a myriad of graphics and sayings about assumptions, including these:

- Never assume anything.
- Assumptions are the termites of relationships. (Henry Winkler)
- Don't be too assuming. It doesn't get you anywhere. (Anne Frank)
- Jumping to conclusions is not actually exercise. (Unknown author)
- Before you "assume," try this crazy method called "asking." (Unknown author)

These quotes/sayings relate to life in general, but in fundraising, they're especially important. As a donor, I have faced other's assumptions about me more times than I can count—and those are the ones that I actually know about. Because of assumptions, donors often feel that they're being "sized up" by fundraisers—and fundraisers often seem to think that the donors aren't aware of this. Whether it's judging them by their attire and accessories, their marital status, the size and location of their home, their profession, or their past donation history, assumptions relating to the donor's "capacity" are made all the time. Sometimes these assumptions are actually correct and things work well. Other times, not so much.

When I ask nonprofit professionals how many millennials they count among their donors and/or board members, I often get a blank stare. For those who actually respond, the answer is usually something like "But they don't have any money yet" or "Do you mean so that we can get them to ask their parents to donate?"

No, I'm asking because, according to a 2019 report on CNBC[6] from Coldwell Banker/Wealth Engine, there are 618,000 millennial millionaires in the US alone—with about 93% of them "worth" between $1 million and $2.5 million. The assumption that they don't have any money yet is, in the case of these particular millennials, incorrect. The assumption that their parents have more money than they do and are more likely than their kids to be donors is also likely to be flawed.

One would assume, then, that the place where most millennial millionaires live is California—or maybe New York. Faulty assumption? Yes! Although the Coldwell Banker/Wealth Engine report does tell us that, yes, 44% of the 618,000 live in California, with many of the rest living in New York, the city with the highest number of millennial millionaires is Traverse City, Michigan.

Surprised? Me too. Now think about how surprised you would be if you looked at someone's clothing—or the size of their home—and assumed, based on those observations, that they were or were not, a "qualified" prospect. Imagine your surprise when you found out that you were completely wrong. It's one thing when you're wrong on the high end (i.e., when the person you thought was wealthy doesn't have the resources you assumed they had), but what about when you're wrong on the low end (when you find out that the person you thought had little or no resources just set up an endowment at your alma mater)?

Don't get me wrong. Information is powerful, and some of the information you have on your prospects can be helpful. However, it's critical that you take those "facts" or data points with a grain (or two) of salt.

And when in doubt, or just to check yourself, remember what I mentioned earlier and **try this crazy method called asking.**

Eight Assumptions

While we're on the topic of assumptions, let's talk about Jeff Brooks and his blog *Future Fundraising Now.* Jeff's postings are not only interesting and accurate, but they are respectful and honest about donors. Integrity and authenticity are what I keep preaching, and Jeff is clearly on the same page.

Jeff posted a great piece called "8 Assumptions You Should Make About Donors."[7] Below—with my comments—are these assumptions.

1. **Donors make decisions with their hearts. Giving them lots of facts does not win them over.** (Yes, hearts, but minds, too. If, as a fundraiser, the person you're pitching to is "just not that into you" after learn-

ing about your organization, then give it a break and go on to the next prospect.)

2. **Donors seek to justify their decisions with facts. A few well-chosen facts can help.** (Emphasis on "well-chosen." If you've done your homework before the pitch meeting, you'll know which facts are likely to be of interest to the prospect.)

3. **Donors are far more interested in what their gift means for them than what it means for you.** (Right! You should be able to leave that call/meeting knowing why a gift might be meaningful for that donor. If you're developing an authentic relationship with the prospect, you should know that answer.)

4. **Donors look for bargains. Anything that makes it feel like their donation does a lot is more attractive.** (This is the "impact" part. Lots of impact with a matching grant? I'm in.)

5. **You can't force donors to do anything. There's no mind control, no secret that makes them give. You have to win each donation.** (By "winning," this doesn't mean you should push me to decide between your organization and another organization. That's bad form and off-putting. And the real "secret" is that you need to listen to the donor and have an honest conversation with them. Donors can usually smell dishonesty and craftiness.)

6. **Donors love to donate.** (Yes! As long as it's done in a way that feels impactful, meaningful, and authentic.)

7. **Donors are afraid your fundraising might be a scam.** (Yes on this, too. See Jon Krakauer's take on this in *Three Cups of Deceit*.)

8. **Most donors like to do what other people are doing.** (Right! Since trust is one of the main factors in giving, it's easier to trust an organization that your friend/colleague has already vetted and donated to.)

Hopefully, more nonprofit advisors like Jeff will jump on the bandwagon and help us make a real and positive change to help NPOs thrive. Jeff also has a great compilation of what he calls "Stupid Nonprofit Ads."[8]

Why Do New Donors Not Renew?

Most new donors have no idea that giving a gift means that you're supposed to "renew" the gift—and, ideally, increase it the following year. I suppose if you give to the "Annual Fund," the implication is clearer, but if I just decide to contribute to your organization when I never have before, I won't know that making that first gift will be interpreted as an implicit commitment to give to you on a regular (annual, at least) basis.

I ran this fact by a few high-level institutional fundraisers at a recent conference, and they were shocked when I told them that there's no way a new donor would know what they're getting into when they happily make a gift to a nonprofit. Why would a donor know that? Is there a person at the organization who tells them that giving "annually" is "the rule" when their first gift is received?

Of course not. The organization is so happy to have a new donor that they don't want to muck it up by telling the donor that there's a long-term expectation now. So imagine how strange it is for a donor, new to giving, to be asked to "increase your annual gift this year" or to "renew your gift." An analogy might be to imagine enjoying a holiday at a lovely bed and breakfast and then getting an email several months later saying, "When you return this year, perhaps you'd like a bigger room?" Who said I was coming back next year?

I've been told many times that I should increase my annual gift when I was never asked if I was interested in giving annually in the first place. Can't I, as a donor, decide to give when I want to?

The worst part of this is when I actually want to give a second gift, and I'm told that it should be a larger dollar amount than the previous gift. (There's a charming story about this at the beginning of *Philanthropy Revolution*. Spoiler alert: it didn't end well.)

Wouldn't it be better to gratefully receive and acknowledge the first gift, nurture a personal relationship with the donor, and only then explain to the donor why annual giving is a lifeline for most nonprofits? Maybe explain how nonprofit budgets work so that the donor can appreciate your educating them—instead of hitting them with an expectation.

I don't think it's a stretch to think that this mismatch of understanding between the new donor and the fundraiser can partially explain the huge drop-off in new donor retention rates. As hundreds of thousands of new donors start giving, we, as a sector, can't afford to turn them off just as they're getting started. Assumptions and expectations on the fundraiser's part are only going to send donors running away from you and your organization.

Think about this: why would a donor, new to giving, know anything about annual renewals, or, for that matter, the donor pyramid, or moves management? All a donor knows is that they're partnering with an organization they believe in and they want to help. Isn't that okay?

Top Tips for Donor Relationships

It's critical, whatever sector you find yourself in (business, education, nonprofits, etc.), **to realize that your success rate will be largely determined by your ability to feel empathy** and show it.

Be cautious when you judge/"size up" a new donor, as it's likely that you don't know their whole story. By making assumptions, you're likely to lose an opportunity for a relationship with them, not to mention a donation.

Don't assume that you know a donor based on their wealth status. Donors, like anyone, are living, breathing individuals with their own personal desires and dreams and personalities. You wouldn't want someone making assumptions about you, would you?

Universities and employers have been doing Google searches on applicants for years. Why are fundraisers hesitant to find out about their prospects before meeting them? Donors will appreciate it if you do your homework.

When you send that short survey to your donors, ask them how often they would like to receive information on your progress. Would they like a newsletter monthly, quarterly, more often, or once a year?

Want to raise more $$ from more donors? Remember the (classic) Maya Angelou quote: "I've learned that people will forget what you said, people will forget what you did, but people will never forget how you made them feel."

CHAPTER 5

DONOR COMMUNICATIONS

Storytelling—Your Organization, Your Mission, and You

Late for a charity event in my San Francisco hotel, I hurriedly left my room and headed downstairs. When I got into the elevator, I turned to the mirrored wall to make sure that my hair looked okay. As I did, I heard the only other passenger in the elevator, a young woman, say, "Oh, can I help you with that?" I thought that was a bit strange, until I looked down and saw that she was holding a basket filled with all sorts of hairdressing tools and products. Turns out she had just left a client; she insisted on fixing my hair. Once outside, she gave my hair a quick spray, and off we went in different directions—but only after I'd asked her for her business card and told her that I'd contact her the next time I was in town.

This was similar to one of those "elevator speeches." It was a quick, to-the-point, meaningful interaction that can only happen in the time it takes for an elevator to reach its destination. It reminded me about one of my frustrations with nonprofits. Coming up, I'll share my reason for that frustration while we look at communication mistakes your organization may be making and how to better share your story to potential and existing donors.

In this chapter, we'll explore:

- Seven rules for email hygiene
- Five gratitude strategies
- Five reasons to write thank-you notes
- The right timing of a thank-you note
- How's your elevator pitch?

The KISS Method

Snail mail, email, text solicitations, phone calls—regardless of the vehicle you use for your fundraising "ask"/pitch, remember to keep it simple.

Just like in an invitation to any kind of event, whether it's a kid's birthday party, an open house, or a gala, you know that you always want to include "who, what, where, when, and why," right? Don't forget to also include an email address and phone number. I know that phone numbers are sometimes tricky when staff are working remotely, but surely there is some way that someone who wants to donate can speak to a real person to get their questions answered.

Ideally, you give a direct phone number (i.e., an office number that "rings through" to a cell or home number), but if that's not possible, then at least ensure that somebody on your team will check messages throughout the day and return calls promptly. (If that "designated staff member" goes on vacation or is otherwise unavailable, make sure that someone else is assigned to monitor the calls on a daily basis.) You all work too hard on getting your solicitations to finally pan out to not have the donation come through because the donor didn't get a question answered.

The same goes for emails. A donor who has decided to donate but has a question pending doesn't want to wait several days or more to get an email response before sending in their payment.

Also, make sure your standard information for payment makes sense. Although many donors pay by credit card, many pay by other means. Make sure alternative options for payment are included on all your solicitations (including your website). If you accept checks or online forms of payment, say so in your collateral. If you are happy to accept donor-advised fund donations, say so—and give the donor the precise information they'll need to make that donation. (Not clearly showing the tax ID number and mailing address for a DAF check on your website—and actually encouraging donations from DAFs—is absolutely leaving money on the table.) If you take appreciated stock, say so, and make it easy for the donor to make that transaction happen.

In addition, here's an important part that many organizations forget. Make sure all your staff, at all levels, and your volunteer or lay leaders too, understand what forms of payment you accept. The first step in receiving a piece of the $234-billion-donor-advised-fund-pie is to actually understand what it is and how the transaction works. You don't need to know the ins and outs tax-wise—you just need to know how to make it easy for the donor to give to your organization.

Finally, now is a good time to do the following exercise (based on the "Secret Shopper" concept). Pretend, just for a few minutes, that you're a donor who wants to give to your organization, and you've never donated to this nonprofit before. Create a persona that makes sense to you—as if you were the donor. Decide if the donor (you) would want to donate online or send in a check or use another method. Then go through the motions and make sure it all works.

Is the online form easy to use? Do the questions on the form make sense? Do you—the company—really need the answers to all the questions you're asking? Are you using that data? Ideally, you would then make a donation—even five dollars—and see what happens. Does a nice "thank you" message appear? Is the language in the acknowledgment to your liking? Does it come in a timely manner? Is your information then put into an appropriate database to encourage future engagement? If there's a phone number, call it and see what a donor would experience. Is the voicemail appropriate? Ideally, here you would leave a friend's name and see how long it takes to get a return call.

Most fundraisers know that recurring (i.e., monthly) donations are a growing piece of the puzzle. Do your website and solicitations always include a request or opportunity to sign up for a recurring donation—and is it easy to find and to sign up for?

Have you ever been in a department store trying to find someone to take your money, only to get frustrated and change your mind about purchasing? The same is true for donations—make it clear, simple, and easy for donors to contribute. If you don't, you're spending time and resources getting a donor teed up, only to have them walk away.

Email and Marketing Hygiene—Seven Things You Need to Know

This is not the kind of hygiene that includes brushing your teeth and washing your hands. Although those are important, this is about email and marketing hygiene. This kind of hygiene is just as important to your business as bathing is to your health.

I know that the term "email hygiene" is often referred to as keeping your database/mailing list "clean" and updated. This version of email hygiene is a bit different, and much more basic.

The word hygiene[1] comes from The Greek word *hygieinē,* and in the ancient world, it meant "sound, healthy, or strong." Applying that definition to nonprofits, we're all using email and other forms of marketing to keep our organizations sound, healthy, and strong. Unfortunately, as a donor, I'm seeing more and more email and marketing materials that are messy, pandering, and off-putting. Some are downright negligent.

Crazy as it may seem, I've received emails and other marketing materials in the last month that exhibited a significant lack of hygiene. From those, I've put together **seven new rules for sending "clean" marketing emails. Breaking any of these rules is likely to result in you turning off an existing or prospective donor.**

Note that you are typically spending the precious resources of time and money to create and send these marketing emails with the goal of securing a donation. Yet making these mistakes (being messy and sloppy) will have the opposite result. Without a detailed look at all aspects of any marketing email before pressing "send," you may be directly sending out something that will have a negative impact on your NGO. In other words, in terms of your organization's reputation and brand, sending that email may be worse than sending no email at all.

Here are my top seven rules for email and marketing hygiene:

1. **Be careful with your recipient list.** It's disrespectful when I, as a donor, receive emails that show the entire distribution of contact information in the cc field. The bcc field is there for a reason! Using an email client that's designed to send mass emails won't allow this to happen. A good double-check is the following: before you send your email, send a test email to yourself and to a few other staff or friends.

2. **Don't break the law.** CAN-SPAM[2] has been around since 2003, and it clearly states that for mass promotional emails there must be a simple, easy-to-find unsubscribe/opt-out option. Most nonprofits comply with

this, and those that use an email marketing service wouldn't be able to send out emails without including this. For me, seeing no unsubscribe option makes me wonder if the organization is legit. In case you think there's no penalty for noncompliance with CAN-SPAM, note that each separate violation is subject to a fine of over $40,000 (USD). Countries outside of the United States have other regulations—some much more stringent. Note that most donors won't be too excited to give to a nonprofit that has broken the law.

3. **Trickery is not a good idea.** Be clear as to who the email is coming from. If you really think that donors/prospects dislike you so much that they won't open an email from you or your organization, why do you think they'd give you money if, instead, you say it's coming from "Management"? If they, for some unknown reason, open your email, they'll still see from the content that it's from you, so what's the point in disguising yourself?

4. **Think about how much is too much to you.** I've heard from several friends and colleagues recently that they received as many as four emails in a single day from a single organization. Think about it in terms of yourself—if you received three emails in a given day that all asked you for money for the same group and you deleted every one, would you magically open the fourth one and then happily send them money? I'd be updating my email settings to block them.

5. **Don't stalk your donor/prospect.** With the advent of new scheduling software like Calendly, I'm receiving emails asking me to schedule my own appointment via the "system" so that the fundraiser can ask me for money. I appreciate the ease of using scheduling apps to make an appointment with my hairdresser, but don't assume I am so excited to hear about your organization that I'm willing to set up the appointment myself. A bit of back-and-forth (i.e., the "getting to know you" phase) is often in order.

6. **Spell-check**—with humans and with software. The number of misspellings I see keeps increasing. Find someone on your staff who's a fanatic speller (and ideally good at grammar) and make sure to include

them on the team to read every mass mailing before you send it out. If you don't have a person like this on your staff, find one.

7. **Don't blame a failed solicitation on technology.** Yesterday my friend received an email solicitation from her alma mater for a one-day alumni fundraising event. They forgot to include an easy-to-find "Give" or "Donate" link. That wasn't the technology's fault, and if you bought a new program for fundraising that doesn't allow you to put a "Donate" button on each page, it's on you for choosing an inappropriate program.

From a donor's perspective, it's so much nicer to think about giving to an NGO based on their mission—but you can't do that if their email hygiene is so deficient that you can't focus on the mission at all. Let's make these rules part of our regular routine and make marketing hygiene a non-issue.

Gratitude & Impact. Gratitude & Impact. Gratitude & Impact. Gratitude & Impact.

Yes, I did mean to write those words over and over again. Why? Because these two words need to be on every fundraiser's mind every time they think, *How can I raise more money?*

There are books and experts and classes and podcasts and more—all telling us how to raise more money to sustain and grow our organizations. That's all great, but without communicating gratitude and impact, donors won't continue giving to you. In the case of younger donors, they might not even *start* giving to you if you aren't able to clearly convey impact.

I don't mean overall impact writ large—I mean the answer to "where did/will my gift go and what did/will it achieve?" I'll break it down in this chapter, as well as look at donor communications. We'll explore not only how your organization might be making first impressions in-person, but also the impression your nonprofit is making online and via mail. Who is the face of your nonprofit? How do donors feel at each point of contact with your organization? Are you clearly conveying gratitude and impact?

Let's start with gratitude. I can't tell you how many times fellow donors have told me they didn't get any type of "thank you" from an organization they gave to—other than a receipt. A receipt with "thank you" written on it is nice, but it's really the lowest level of, well, manners. It has no life to it, takes almost no time, and doesn't recognize the recipient as an individual human being.

I know that everyone reading this knows these things innately, but when faced with organizational bureaucracies and limited resources, somehow we decide that the minimum expression of gratitude (or none at all) is just fine—as long as money is coming in from somewhere.

This is not okay. Every one of your donors deserves some form of gratitude. Without a request for more money. A few years ago, I learned about some colleges and universities calling non-donor alumni regularly for as long as ten years post-graduation (with zero results). Could we maybe move some of those (non-performing) resources over to your new donors to express gratitude? Can't we take a moment now to call or email your newer donors just to say thank you?

My friend and colleague Claire Axelrad wrote on this subject but applied it to annual reports in her article "Transform Annual Reports into Gratitude Reports for the Best ROI."[3] I encourage you to read her full article. In it, she gives the "top five gratitude report strategies." They include:

1. Tell a story with the donor at the center—tell emotionally resonant stories
2. Use pictures worth 1,000 words—try photos to grab attention and keep it
3. Inspire action—what's the purpose of your report?
4. Cut the crap—find out what your donors like and get rid of what they don't
5. Take it online—use links, video, and dynamic elements

As far as conveying impact, we tend to offer broad, overly wordy, nonspecific answers to the question of "Where did my money go?" Almost always, that information is laden with requests for additional donations. As a donor (remember, you're a donor as well), don't you feel that the messaging fades into the background the moment you're asked for more money? We also know this doesn't work long-term.

Remember the postcard I received from a political candidate I supported thanking me for a donation by succinctly telling me what my donation allowed her to achieve. It made me feel glad to know that my gift meant something. That rarely happens, though. Witness the ever-declining numbers of donors over the last several years:

According to Independent Sector's Quarterly Health Report[4] (December 2022), the number of dollars given to nonprofits as of the second quarter of 2022 is higher than the same time period in 2021, but the number of donors and retention of donors declined. A Lilly School of Philanthropy study from July 2021 revealed that where 66.2% of American households gave charitable donations in 2000, only 49.6% of US households made a charitable contribution in 2018—a drop of almost 17 percentage points during that time period. Although giving increased a bit during the first year of the pandemic, the number quickly went back to where it was pre-pandemic, and the decline seems to have continued since. According to the Independent Sector report, this drop resumed a downward trend that was seen for more than ten years pre-pandemic.

The largest declines in donors from Q2 2021 to Q2 2022 were among those who gave less than $100 (−17.4%) and $101–$500 (−8.0%). This sub-$500 segment of donors accounts for 86% of all donors and about 98% of the decline in donors.

There are many reasons for the decline, but included in those reasons are the facts that (1) trust in nonprofits continues to erode and (2) many nonprofits still don't see the urgency of bringing new and younger donors into the mix. Do our gratitude practices today—especially relative to newer and younger donors—convey that these people are critically important to our success? Not so much.

So our gratitude is expressed almost exclusively to our current, larger donors, and our "impact reports" rarely offer a succinct answer to that question of "Where did my money go?" Both of those responses do little more than continue the cycle of focusing a huge percentage of our time on our current, older, wealthy donors, with next to nothing focused on the "new guys." Is it sustainable, or even remotely prudent, to rely on only older, wealthy donors for our ongoing sector health? I can't think of any business sector where that would make sense.

I love the way that "The Giving Environment: Understanding Pre-Pandemic Trends in Charitable Giving"[5] responds to this data. The conclusion of the report reads:

> America's rapidly changing social and economic landscape provides both an opportunity and a challenge for the philanthropic sector to evolve beyond traditional fundraising methods. **To circumvent the declining giving rate and to inspire the next generation, nonprofits will need to adopt new practices for tomorrow's donors.**

There you have it.

Gratitude and the Corresponding Secretary

There has been a fair amount of discussion about saying "thank you" to donors among fundraisers lately. There is a strange sentiment on the part of nonprofits (and a donor or two) that saying "thank you" is inappropriate, and even pandering. I strongly disagree, but I suppose everyone is entitled to their opinion. (As a donor, it's safe to assume that I will not be giving money to any organization or fundraiser that subscribes to the "no-need-to-say-thank-you" school of thinking.)

Let's just assume that you, my reader, agree with me that saying "thank you" is very important. In fact, I found this piece in *Forbes*'s Lifestyle section called "Five Reasons to Write Thank-You Notes,"[6] and I recommend that everyone read it. Author Nancy Olson's five reasons are:

- It's the right thing to do.
- Jimmy Fallon does it. (!)
- It sets you apart.
- Gratitude is good for the brain.
- Handwritten letters perpetuate a very important part of our culture.

Agreed on all counts. I want to focus on handwritten letters. Several years ago, I was on the board of a nonprofit that had a wonderful woman on staff. Her main job was to manage the senior staff person's calendar, to write certificates, and to compose and write thank-you letters. She had been at the nonprofit for decades, and there was some concern that the organization's resources shouldn't be used for someone to do those seemingly archaic tasks.

I was definitely in the minority when I suggested that the organization modify this person's job description to anoint her as the official "hostess" and "corresponding secretary" of the organization. In past decades, the corresponding secretary was a real thing, and that person actually was in charge of, well, correspondence. The thought was that having someone 100% responsible for making sure that people are welcomed appropriately and thanked in a timely and thoughtful manner would have a positive impact on membership and the organization's "brand." This woman handwrote the most personal, lovely thank-you notes that I've ever seen, and I, as a member, had felt a little thrill when I saw her handwriting on a letter addressed to me. She also made thoughtful phone calls to members when needed, and these were equally lovely.

The National Council of Nonprofits has an excellent article called "Showing Gratitude to Donors."[7] The piece suggests that "expressing regular and authentic gratitude to the donors, volunteers (including board members), and others who support your organization's mission is one of the most important things you can do."

Most importantly, it goes on to say, "Thanking donors meaningfully has multiple benefits. It helps move your development program from one that is transactional—where each 'ask' and response is a separate event—to one that is relationship-based . . . The way donors are thanked can also have a significant impact on the likelihood that they will give again."

That "giving again" part is, obviously, very important, as only about 20% of first-time donors give a second time (to the same organization), and only about 45% of repeat donors continue giving to the same organization. We need to find a way—or several ways—to improve on these numbers (which have been in those ranges for years).

Of course, it would be lovely and ideal if every fundraiser wrote their own thoughtful, personalized thank-you notes in a timely fashion, but in today's busy world, that's rarely the case. Bring back the "corresponding secretary"—or at least add that function to the member of your admin staff who's best at this bygone practice—and give your organization a great way to increase retention and revenue.

I'm often asked if thank-you notes need to be handwritten, or if emails, or even phone calls, are okay. The answer is "it depends." The handwritten note has a personal quality as well as being different and special, but any level of thank you is better than no thank you at all. I happen to love personal phone calls that express gratitude and don't ask for another donation in the next breath, but I usually save the handwritten notes. I'm happy with any of the above, as long as the sentiment is timely and feels sincere.

One final word on this: it's totally okay to ask a donor how they prefer to be thanked. You'll be surprised that most have an opinion on this, and if you really do have a relationship with that donor (as you should), they'll usually tell you how they feel about being thanked. Pay attention to their answer and be sure to note their preferences in your database.

Black and Blue and Read All Over

The land of philanthropy-oriented social media has been, well, "atwitter" lately with discussions about ink colors on fundraising materials. As a donor, I'm both pleased and annoyed about this discussion.

I'm pleased because one of the categories of "fundraising materials" being discussed is thank-you notes. Just the idea that fundraisers are concerned about the presentation of their thank-you notes tells me that they think these notes are really, really important. But are handwritten thank-you notes important at all? Are donors more likely to give more money and/or more often because they received a handwritten thank-you note? This is where I get annoyed.

As I mention later in the book, my son and I are fortunate to have developed a bit of a relationship with the head of a nonprofit called Folding@home[8]—an organization that uses large amounts of data to aid in researching and finding cures for cancer, COVID, and other illnesses. The relationship was started not because of a handwritten thank-you note, but because of a heartfelt thank-you email.

Now that I've read the various posts about blue ink over black, or using an ink color that matches the time of year, I'm reminded that everyone has their own desires and feelings about thank-you notes. Which is great. Except . . . what about the time, thought, and hand-wringing that goes along with thinking about the color and quality of a thank-you note? Does it really make a difference? Are donors more likely to continue giving, or increase their giving, because of the hue of ink used on a handwritten note?

As a donor, my guess is that it doesn't make that much of a difference. Even if the ink color moves the needle a bit more toward a gift or future engagement, I don't think it's a major factor in anyone's giving.

If you do choose to write a note to a donor, is it important to use an ink color that makes it clear that the note is actually handwritten? Absolutely. Is it important to spend precious time thinking about ink colors? With limited resources in the nonprofit world, I don't think pondering ink colors is time well spent.

As a donor, I think that all this discussion is missing the critical point. **The critical point—the piece that really, really counts in terms of your relationship with a donor—is the timing of the thank-you "note."** Whether that thank you comes via email, handwritten letter, or carrier pigeon, it doesn't matter one bit if the timing isn't right. Simply said, the thank you must be sent to the donor as quickly as possible. I usually suggest that a thank-you note must be sent within forty-eight hours, but at a recent conference I attended, another panelist strongly recommended that the note be sent the same day. That panelist is probably right.

In terms of timing, should we even be discussing "snail mail" thank-you notes at all? With the changes in the post office—and standard mail delivery times taking five to seven days or more—is it really worth waiting for the mail to deliver your thank-you message? A lot of annoyance and even bad can happen if a donor doesn't get a thank-you message in fewer than five to seven days.

Don't get me wrong—I think that a handwritten thank-you note is lovely, if only because we get so few of them in general. If you want to write one, go right ahead, but make that your more formal follow-up thank you. The first thank you should be immediate—within a day or two—and it should be a phone call, video message, or standard email. It's all about the timing.

Another super-important piece to this has to do with the message I give everyone when talking about the donor's perspective. Don't assume that the donor will respond one way or another because you wrote a lovely thank-you note. Assuming gets you into trouble.

Elevators

At the opening of this chapter, I mentioned my encounter in a San Francisco hotel elevator and how that exchange reminded me of one of my frustrations with nonprofits. For-profits, especially startups looking for funding, are skilled at making the most of any interaction once they identify a potential funder or customer. They practice over and over again, making sure their "elevator speech" is brief, compelling, and clear, hoping it results in the exchange of business cards (and ideally, the promise of a future meeting.)

But nonprofits are another story altogether. Often, people associated with charitable organizations have trouble succinctly describing what their organization does. Whether it's the executive director (ED), senior management, general staff, or a board member, everyone who has a stake in a nonprofit should have a perfect "elevator speech" at the ready—always. It's shocking how often I ask someone in passing what they do and I hear "Oh, I work for a nonprofit," or "I sit on a few boards." Why do I have to then ask them what nonprofit they work for? Or what the boards are that they sit on?

If you spend time—whether it be work time or volunteer time (as in board service)—why would you want to waste any opportunity to promote your organization? If opportunities present themselves in brief encounters with potential partners or funders, you don't have the luxury of being coy or evasive. In fact, doing so is a disservice to the organization you serve.

This scenario happens enough that it makes me wonder if people are embarrassed that they work for—or are associated with—a nonprofit. I hope that's not true and that the lack of a well-honed elevator speech is just a matter of an organization not teaching its people how to do it.

So, in the spirit of not missing any other opportunities—whether it be in a real elevator or elsewhere—learn from those startup mavericks and get your perfect elevator speech written, refined, and ready to go. Don't arrive at the lobby without it.

Top Tips for Communications

Ask ALL your donors how they would like to be communicated with (text, email, snail mail, phone, etc.) by sending/emailing them a short multiple-choice survey.

Think about your Call to Action. Can it include volunteering, or non-monetary participation? Donors will still give, but they'll feel like your relationship with them is fuller, and more than just financial.

It's important to ask your donors how they like to be thanked. Send them a brief survey and ask them how they want to be thanked. Make it multiple-choice and include options for anonymous, publicly, handwritten card, etc.

We learn when we're toddlers to say thank you. When you receive a donation (or when someone volunteers!) don't forget to say thank you. If you want to write a note, great. Email—great. Phone call—terrific. The point is, to do it right away!

Imagine a donor's surprise when you thank them via a short, personal video made just for them. It takes under a minute to do. Try it!

It's unacceptable, not to mention very annoying, to send out a mass email solicitation without an unsubscribe link. It's even more annoying when you've clearly purchased the list.

CHAPTER 6

EVENTS

How to Approach Prospects—Think Cocktail Party!

I received yet another invitation to a gala, and it's hard not to hold my breath as I open the envelope. Even before I open the envelope (yes, generally still snail mail), I see the return address with the name of the organization that the gala is supporting. Usually, my initial thought is *Oh, I do love that organization—let's look at the details.* But more and more often, the honoree's name is listed just under the name of the organization.

At this point—even before opening the envelope—I'm in a quandary. I like the organization, but I have no idea who the honoree is. Or, at other times, I'll see that I really like and respect the honoree, but I don't care for the organization. What to do? I haven't even opened the envelope to see the date of the event, how much is being charged, who's included, a handwritten note telling me I should come, and if there's entertainment that I'm interested in. Cue the moment where I start hoping that I'm already booked on that date. Let's look at some dos and don'ts when it comes to hosting events for your nonprofit.

In this chapter, we'll cover:

- An old way to bring new and interesting people together
- How to host a salon
- The pros and cons of galas
- Four new ideas for a successful gala
- Don't make your attendees feel like lurkers

Salons—A Centuries-Old Tradition

Before I was so focused on philanthropy, I had been invited to a few small fundraising events in people's homes to learn about organizations that needed help—typically for nonprofits, politicians, or political causes. They were lovely events, and the invitation almost always suggested that the event was not necessarily meant to raise money, but instead to help us (the invited guests) learn about the group and its cause. It was implied that the organization hoped we would be so impressed with their presentation that we would be compelled to donate to them.

Years later, I found myself in the fortunate position of owning a home with a good-sized living room and a large backyard—both perfect for charitable events. It was a given that we would use these spaces in the most productive way possible, ideally helping organizations and causes we had a keen interest in. Our family also realized that not everyone was aware of the issues we were concerned about.

Learning what a nonprofit does—understanding the issues, the context, and the need for the organization's work—is critical to someone becoming interested in being a donor or supporter. You can't raise money if a donor doesn't understand what you do. With that in mind, we decided that educating our community about the issues we care about was step number one in helping beloved organizations grow and thrive. And we would do this by hosting various nonprofits in our living room.

We learned that this idea—educating those around us by bringing impressive social leaders into our home—had been done for centuries, starting in Europe in the sixteenth century. It's commonly understood that the purpose of salons, although varied in content, is to increase the knowledge of the participants through conversation.[1] Philanthropy ("patronage") was often a big part of these gatherings, and whether that patronage was to support a writer, an artist, or a cause, these events were—and continue to be—an important part of the picture for successful nonprofit organizations.

The interesting thing is that more people don't do these. It's really not difficult to host a salon (or, if you prefer, a "party," "soiree," or "small fundraiser"). Ask a nonprofit you care about if they would like to expand their reach—they should be thrilled that you're asking—and then invite some friends, have them invite some friends, and pull up some chairs in your living room. Joan Garry, in her "10 Rules for a Successful Small Fundraiser,"[2] provides a terrific and useful checklist to ensure that the event is a success.

Note that depending on the nonprofit, especially for organizations that are just getting going or that don't have presence in your geographic area, your event may need to be a "friend-raiser" instead of a fundraiser. And that might be okay, because you need to educate others, create recognition, and then build a base before being able to raise real money.

To that end, it's important to note that a salon should be an important part of an organization's "awareness strategy." There are loads of articles about awareness campaigns, and they often include a lot of online components. However, person-to-person awareness, with real people learning from the leaders and/or beneficiaries of a nonprofit, brings a reality to the picture that can directly support the building of the foundation for your organization's growth.

If you're ready to jump in and host a salon, here are some tips to ensure the event's success, courtesy of this passionate and longtime salon host. Be well organized and prepared, down to the smallest detail—but know that this is not a fully comprehensive list:

- If you're using tech, check it at least an hour before the event begins (this includes microphones, speakers, laptops, projection equipment, etc.).
- Decide if you want name tags and, if so, have them printed and ready to go. Also, a sign-in sheet is a good idea—and a way to confirm attendance and capture email addresses.
- Determine if you will impose any health restrictions, and if you do, communicate that to the guests well in advance.
- If you want to be able to listen to the presentation (and I highly recommend you do), have someone there to serve refreshments and clean up. Make sure the speaker has water available.
- If there's going to be an "ask" (for money, volunteers, connections, or anything else), decide in advance who will make that ask and at what point during the event it will happen. Don't try to get the group together again after they've finished listening to the presentation—it won't work.

- Manage expectations with the guests and the nonprofit before you send out a single invitation. Is this "friend-raising" only, or will there be a request for money?
- Serve some type of food and drink. Finger food is great. Cocktails are not necessary, but wine, soft drinks, and tea and coffee are appreciated.
- Remember that the focus here is for the guests to learn together—this isn't a party and it doesn't need to be "fancy" at all. When in doubt, tone it down.
- Determine an end time and stick to it. Be clear at the outset how the "run of show" will happen, including the approximate length of the presentation, confirmation that there will be plenty of time for questions, and the time you will adjourn. Your guests will appreciate it.

A side benefit of these salons is that you get to hone your pitch skills while getting to know your community a bit better. It's a win-win. Try it!

It's My Party

I'm not sure when the word "gala" began to be used for charity fundraisers, but my guess is that the word "fundraiser" was too in-your-face to successfully get people to come to a "party." I've seen the description "Gala Fundraiser," which is more accurate, but rarely used. Regardless, most nonprofits at some point have a gala. Most larger nonprofits have them annually. And some of them make lots of money. In fact, for many organizations, the gala is the biggest fundraising event/program/project of the year. But consider this: a large number of galas don't actually make money. This fact seems to be one of the well-known secrets of the fundraising world—one that nobody wants to talk about.

A recent *Forbes* piece, "How to Organize the Perfect Fundraising Gala,"[3] does a great job of discussing the pros and cons of putting on galas (they also get into very helpful details about the steps required to make it successful). One of the comments made in the article is to only have a gala "if you don't have another, 'less-costly' way to activate donors." Another great comment in the article, when discussing the high cost of food and drink at these events, is to make sure you "... generate cash for your mission, not your chicken."

Galas have their own special type of challenges associated with them. I'll start by clarifying what the "standards" for galas are today. First, the organization will choose someone to be "honored." The qualifications for that someone are that they will be able to market hard to their personal mailing list and secure a big donation from their company (or from them personally, depending on the honoree). Sometimes there are two or three of these "honorees," each with their own mailing list and large donation capability. Sometimes there is top-level entertainment, but less frequently than you might think. Almost always, there is a large venue booked, a committee of volunteers formed, and either an in-house event team, an outside event planner, or a combination of the two. Sometimes there's an "ad book" (either "digital" or in print) and sometimes there's a silent auction. Other than a few outliers here and there, these are the standard components of today's fundraising galas.

I used to think that all gala honorees were people who had given lots of time and/or money to the organization. Happily, many of them are just that. But a decent amount of them are people whose companies have paid for them to be "honored" as a promotional tool. One board that I was on let pretty much anyone be an "honoree" as long as their company paid $50,000 up front.

Let's say that the above doesn't bother you, because money is money, and however the gala is financed, as long as it makes bank, is just fine. You'll attend or not attend, but you'll buy a ticket or a table because you love the organization and just want them to be successful. Fine. I do that too. But it's often fraught.

When I've purchased those tickets or tables for some events, I'll often bring guests who I think might enjoy knowing about the organization. This has backfired more than once, when the gala is ridiculously long, painfully boring, "guilts" people—in this public setting—into making a gift, or includes inappropriate or "in-crowd" speeches. The result of any or all of this is that my guests vow they'll never have anything to do with that organization.

But let's assume I don't bring a guest and that the program is professional and fine. During most galas, there is a moment in the program where the organization touts the amount of money that the gala appears to be making from that event. Did you know that the vast majority of those announcements, where someone senior in the organization talks about all the money they just made, are speaking about gross dollars raised as opposed to net dollars raised?

I've started a bit of a routine with many of the organizations I support. As I congratulate them on the large "take" from their event, I also ask them if the amount "raised" is gross or net. The answer I get is somewhere between "I don't know" and "We don't have the final numbers in yet" and (my personal favorite) a blank stare, suggesting that the person I'm speaking with doesn't know the difference. (For those new to this, a simplified explanation is that the "gross" is the total amount received, and the "net" is the amount left over after all expenses are paid.)

Somewhere in that conversation, or in conversations following my initial query, I find out that the net amount raised is a small fraction of the gross. That's because these events require a huge amount of resources, in terms of hard costs as well as staff costs and opportunity costs, and sometimes the "net dollars raised" is closer to, well, a very small amount of money.

It's unusual to find an organization that includes internal staff costs (much less opportunity costs) in their final summation of the amount of money that their gala raised (i.e., the net amount.) Why is that? Is that because the event was a fun social thing that provided great promotion of the nonprofit—and the net amount raised was less important? Is it because "everyone loves a party"? Maybe. All I can say here is that it breaks my heart to see how incredibly hard staff and volunteers work to put on these events, only to contribute a pittance to the bottom line.

As a board member and a donor, I want to know that the organization I'm supporting is doing all they can to stay "on mission" and to use every penny wisely. All too often, the "party" takes over everything for a lengthy period of time, and I can't help but wonder if the mission—or the health of the organization—suffers during that period.

Knowing all of the above, some organizations have decided to add innovation to the gala model. Here are several "new ideas" relative to galas that I've seen used very successfully:

1. Query your database, look at the demographics of your donors and prospects, and get a sense of the level of interest in the typical "rubber-chicken" gala. You'll likely find that some of your donors/prospects love these parties, but many of your donors/prospects really aren't comfortable at them. (This is often generational, at least in part.) Cedars-Sinai Medical Center did this type of study and determined that a number of their constituents wanted something more casual, family oriented, low priced, and fun. The resulting event, "Rock for Research," has quickly become the event that the Board of Governors (who the event is catered to) most enjoy and look forward to. And it makes money, too!

2. Mandate an end time for your events, and honor it 100%. I developed even more admiration for the Liberty Hill Foundation when I found out they have a hard-and-fast rule that every gala ends at 9:30 p.m. (Other organizations, take note!)

3. Give the recipient of the invitation an easy out—one that's a "win-win" all around. Make it super easy and honorable for the recipient to not attend the event by instead underwriting tickets for staff, supporters, grantees, students, and volunteers. If a donor does this, remember to refrain from telling or writing to them that you "missed them at the event" or "hope to see you next year." Just say "thank you!"

4. During and after the event, drive home the organization's mission and note involvement opportunities. Yes—work to raise money to sustain and grow your organization. But also make sure not to waste an opportunity: while every person in that room may not be a prospective donor (or bigger donor), they can all provide some type of nonfinancial support. Whether it be volunteering, telling others about the nonprofit and what you accomplish (including younger people!), or providing a resource or referral, use the event's existence as a broad promotional vehicle. I love emails received within twenty-four hours of a gala, reminding me of the highlights of the event, thanking me for attending (or contributing), and letting me know how I can help further the organization's mission. A video clip or two is always great too!

Leaving Baby in a Corner

Several years ago, I was invited to a major donor event held by a long-standing Jewish institution that I had supported (let's call them "JI"). The event was relatively small (only about fifty to seventy-five people in attendance), and invited guests were those who gave the highest-level annual gift to the organization. Although I had given a substantial gift to this NPO, I was not in that highest category.

So why was I invited? I was on the guest speaker's guest list because the speaker, Chelsea Clinton, was representing her organization, the Clinton Global Initiative. The CGI invited me because they were soliciting me as a donor and they knew I'd be interested in meeting Ms. Clinton. They also knew that I was a major donor in the community (and to the JI), and that I would likely know the other folks in the room, so I'd feel comfortable. All nice, right?

You would think so, until I arrived at the event. I checked into the event without any issue and proceeded to the ballroom to find my table. (The program included a sit-down dinner, so the tables were arranged accordingly.) There were no table assignments or "reserved" signs, and nobody greeted me to show me a seat, so I just found a seat at an empty table and waited for the program to begin.

Imagine my surprise when another donor asked me to leave the table, claiming that the table was his. Strange, but okay . . .

As it was a small room—and there were a number of staff milling around—I thought someone would see what was happening and find me another seat. Nope. Nada. The presentation was beginning, and I didn't want to be chased from yet another table, so I stood at the back of the room—still assuming that someone from the staff would notice me and find me a seat.

Still nothing. Despite my substantial gifts in the past, this particular organization completely ignored me. (Silly me—I thought that we had a "relationship"!) Eventually, I gave up and went home. What do you think happened the next time JI solicited me for a gift? You know the answer.

For all the incredible hard work that fundraisers do to recruit and retain donors, my relationship with JI ended during the hour that I was at the venue. The lesson? Make sure your guests are greeted! It doesn't have to be a long conversation. A couple of words and a smile will do it.

And then . . . on a number of Zoom calls, I realized that I felt that same unnoticed/back-of-the-room sensation—almost like I was a lurker. Why? I realized that I had been personally welcomed at some online/virtual events in the past weeks by just a quick "Welcome!" in the private chat box, but not in others. It then became clear that donors, potential donors, and volunteers are often ignored by organizations they support—online. Not intentionally, I'm sure, but because we haven't successfully fine-tuned these virtual events quite yet.

It was at that moment I remembered the unfortunate event at the CGI/JI dinner. I realized that when we moved to Zoom for almost everything, we forgot some basic manners. If the event I was participating in via Zoom was happening IRL (in real life) and I was sitting at a dinner table or walking into a venue, someone from the staff would absolutely have welcomed me, as well as all guests. That "working the room" thing that is a part of every event in some way (greeting guests by going around a table, shaking hands at a cocktail party, introducing people to each other) somehow didn't fully transfer to the Zoom world as well as one might have hoped.

The good news is that this is easily remedied. Quick notes in a chat box saying "Welcome, Lisa, so glad you're joining us!" or "Hi, I hope you're doing well" cost nothing except a few seconds of time, but go a long way in making the recipient/guest feel that their presence is noticed. It will eliminate the "lurker" feeling and will also likely reduce drop-offs.

Whether online or offline, greetings and acknowledgments just make people feel seen and appreciated. We're pretty good at doing them in an offline event, but as online events, in some form, are here to stay, we need to add this small addition to our repertoire.

Top Tips for Events

Think of digital platforms for events as an opportunity, as opposed to a poor substitute for "the real thing." Research shows that virtual events (done well) are here to stay, but that hybrid events (both virtual and in-person) are the most successful in terms of fundraising and viewership.

Please don't send a "thanks to your contribution, we raised xx dollars" email for an event I didn't go to or give to. Doing so makes me concerned that the organization may be dysfunctional. Better to write "thanks to the support of our community, we raised . . ."

Engagement, anyone? For online events or meetings where you're hosting donors, prospects, or volunteers, welcome each attendee individually via private chat—it makes a difference.

Greet your guests! At in-person events, make sure every guest is acknowledged. Don't expect them to find their own seat.

Consider all costs involved in your event. In order to be a success, an event needs to be engaging, informative, and inspiring. It also needs to be profitable.

CHAPTER 7

VOLUNTEERS

The Donors You Don't See

I've been writing and speaking for years now about the way volunteers are thought of by many nonprofits; many of them are thought of as second-class citizens. Although many nonprofits still put volunteers in their own little box, keeping them separate from donors, I'm pleased to see that standard changing a bit. Maybe it's because giving numbers are declining and nonprofits are looking wherever they can for help and more donors? I'm not sure, but it's great to see that some leaders at NPOs are beginning to realize that volunteers are an extremely important part of any charitable organization.

Why are volunteers an important (I say critical) part of your organization? Why do we need to "sound the alarm" about this recruiting issue? Let's look at volunteers through a wider lens and consider some stats on this often-overlooked part of your organization.

In this chapter, we'll cover:

- The return on investment of a strong volunteer group
- Surprising statistics about volunteers
- Why volunteers volunteer, and why they quit

The Donors Right in Front of You

I've noticed a number of articles lately lamenting the decline of volunteers. A recent article in the *Chronicle of Philanthropy* was titled, "Why and How Charities Should Revive a Declining but Vital Resource . . . Volunteers."[1] In the article, Jennifer Bennett of VolunteerMatch says ". . . charities that made few efforts to remain connected to volunteers in 2020 and 2021 will spend years rebuilding volunteer programs." She adds, "It's not just a lack of institutional knowledge, but a rupture in the relationship. Charities that laid off volunteer managers and didn't have a strategy for keeping the communication lines open with volunteers are back to starting from scratch."

Much of this happened because when COVID started, many nonprofits, faced with an existential threat, panicked. For a large number of them, the panic resulted in—no surprise—cutting the non-revenue-producing staff. Volunteer coordinators are often thought of as "nice to have" rather than essential.

But are volunteers really nonessential and/or non-revenue producing? The article continues by saying, "It's also a missed opportunity, some experts point out. **The return on investment in a strong volunteer program—primarily, the donated work that organizations might otherwise have to pay for—often far exceeds the money they spend on oversight and salaries for volunteerism professionals.** And a talented cadre of volunteers can help depleted charities continue to serve clients at a time when many organizations are struggling to fill open positions."

In another section of the same article, Volunteer Iowa's Michelle Raymer says, "For every dollar you're saving, you're losing even more from having fewer volunteers coming into your organization." The article goes on to say, "Robust volunteering programs are also valuable because of the close association between volunteers and donors. **A person who becomes familiar with an organization through volunteering is likely to eventually become a donor.**"

Is the goal for a volunteer to eventually become a donor? (In this case, "donor" means a financial donor.) According to the Global Trends in Giving Report (2020), 85% of volunteers are also donors to the same nonprofit they volunteer for. If that's true, should our goal really be to get even more of the volunteers to "become donors"?

VolunteerHub says, "Volunteers are 66% more likely to donate financially to the organization they support than those who do not volunteer their time." In terms of dollars, VolunteerMatch[2] found that Americans who volunteer at nonprofits give an average of ten times more money to charity than people who don't volunteer.

Here are a few other head-turning stats:

1. There are over one billion volunteers globally, and approximately sixty-three million Americans volunteer annually.

2. In 2019, 77.9 million American adults volunteered 5.8 billion hours, with a corresponding economic value of about $147 billion. (Note that that amount does not include cash contributions.)

3. Per a Fidelity Charitable[3] report, 87% of volunteers say there is an overlap between their volunteer and financial support, and **50% of volunteers say they give more financial support because they volunteer.**

4. Also, per the same Fidelity report, high-net-worth volunteers give up to ten times more money than non-volunteers, and most donate to the organizations in which they are involved.

5. Want to engage younger donors? Many studies show that younger donors (millennials, Gen Z, etc.) are much more likely to give to an organization that they trust, and **they "check out" the organizations they're interested in by volunteering.**

6. The 2016 Millennial Impact Report showed that 72% of the millennials studied had volunteered in the year prior to the report and 84% made a donation to a nonprofit.

7. As many of you know (but it bears repeating—often), $68 trillion will be transferred to the younger generation in the United States over the next twenty-five years. It will be the largest wealth transfer in history.

So what does all this tell us? It tells us that putting volunteers into one "box" and putting donors into another mutually exclusive box isn't helpful. In fact, the new donors who can sustain our organizations long-term may be right in front of us—and we just don't see them.

This isn't only true for young people. Look at bequests, where receiving "surprise" gifts from donors that aren't on your "major donor" list is a common occurrence. Most nonprofits are surprised to find out that although the bequest donor wasn't on their "list," they had been volunteering for their organization. And you had no idea they existed.

Can donors and volunteers both be thought of as significant partners with (and supporters of) your nonprofit? You bet.

An October 5, 2021, blog entry by philanthropist Jane Leighty Justis[4] reinforces my point. The Leighty Foundation funded and directed a five-year initiative to increase the capacity of nonprofit organizations in the Colorado Springs area. The results clearly demonstrate, as Leighty Justis explains, "**a strong connection between organizations that operate with volunteer engagement as a core strategy for mission accomplishment, and the overall health and effectiveness of the organization.**" Points of Light[5]—the largest network of volunteer-mobilizing organizations in the world—confirms the critical impact of robust volunteer programs on nonprofits.

For example:

- Organizations that fundamentally leverage volunteers and their skills to accomplish their missions are significantly more adaptable, sustainable, and capable of going to scale.
- Organizations that effectively engage volunteers are equally as successful in accomplishing their mission as their peers without volunteers, but at almost half the median budget.
- Effective volunteer engagement has been shown in some cases to reap up to a six-dollar return on every dollar invested when considering the financial value of volunteer involvement.

Jane Leighty Justis puts it this way: "**Volunteers are vastly underused, yet they're a virtually unlimited renewable resource.**" According to the research shown above, the majority of these volunteers both volunteer and donate. But what about our boxes, then, with their corresponding staff, databases, and (often) separate resources? How can this be?

As my new friend Tim Arnold says, "Take a deep breath and say, 'Hey, both of these things can be true.'" I know it's not the way you might have been taught, but donors and volunteers don't only coexist; people can be donors, volunteers, or both at the same time—and that's not only okay, it's terrific! When someone is both a donor and a volunteer, we should celebrate these "hybrid supporters" as opposed to being befuddled by their existence.

Let's change the way we work with everyone and anyone who is inspired by the work we do—and let's stop needing them to stay in their "assigned" categories. Let's start thinking of all our supporters as human beings who want us to succeed in our mission. The result—lower costs, increased revenue, and fulfilled supporters—can dramatically transform our organizations for the better.

Why Are We Surprised That It's Tough to Find Volunteers?

A February 7, 2023, article in *The Chronicle of Philanthropy* is titled "Nonprofit Leaders Want More Volunteers but Say It Is Tough to Recruit Them."[6] It states that ". . . nearly 70% of nonprofit leaders surveyed said volunteers were a very worthy investment for nonprofits in 2022 versus 43% in a related survey in 2019."

Most of us know that volunteers help offset costs and provide additional resources, talent, and time. What we often **don't** think about is that they're often donors as well. Need convincing? Here's all you need to know:

1. Volunteers are 66% more likely to donate financially[7] to the organization they support than those who do not volunteer their time.
2. Americans who volunteer their time and skills to NPOs donate an average of ten times more money[8] to charity than people who don't volunteer.
3. Younger donors, thinking about their charitable path, are "checking out" nonprofits they're interested in giving to by **first volunteering**. Many of them feel they can best understand how an organization works and how "legit" they are by volunteering for them first.

Assuming that piques your interest, let's now think about why volunteers don't want to "sign up" or continue volunteering. A wonderful article from the people at Track it Forward[9] (a volunteer tracking and information company) says it best as they look at "**Why Volunteers Volunteer and Why Volunteers Quit.**" Some key points:

1. They volunteer "because they have a personal tie to the mission, but they quit because they're unaware of their impact." (And/or they don't see the impact of the organization at all.)
2. They volunteer "because they want to feel important and have a sense of purpose, but they quit because they don't feel recognized."
3. They volunteer "because they want to build new skills, and then they quit because they're not given opportunities to do new things in the organization."

I'll add a few more reasons why volunteers quit (and don't volunteer again) from my experience:

1. They volunteer because they feel they have something to contribute to the organization (usually some type of expertise), but they quit because that expertise isn't being used or even acknowledged.
2. They volunteer to be able to better understand the culture of the organization (i.e., they want to trust the organization before they give money), and they quit because they see that the nonprofit is dysfunctional, wasteful, and/or unproductive.
3. They volunteer because they believe in the organization and its mission, and they quit because they don't feel that the organization believes in (or respects) them.
4. They volunteer because it feels personally satisfying to "give back" in that way, but they quit because they spend a lot of time standing around waiting for instructions, and they (often) don't see the value of the work they're doing.
5. They volunteer to get a firsthand view into the people who run the nonprofit, but they quit because they never have a chance to meet them.
6. They volunteer because they want to support the organization fully and are starting out learning the landscape by volunteering, but they quit because, despite the obvious need for more funding, they're never asked for a donation because they're not in the "donor group."

If you're still having trouble seeing the opportunities missed by minimizing the impact and potential of your volunteers, think about the bequests that you've received. A good number of them come from volunteers who nobody in the finance/development office recognizes the name of—and they're often very large amounts of money.

There's a terrific report by the Stelter Company called "The Secret Giver"[10] that looks at the statistics of untapped prospect groups. As you read it, think about your volunteers and how dedicated they are to your organization and mission. Chances are there are several "Secret Givers" right under your nose.

When you keep your donors and volunteers in separate (and often unequal) boxes because you think "volunteers don't give," you're doing a disservice to your organization (as well as to those volunteers and donors). The time is now to change how you think of (and interact with) your volunteers. Carpe diem!

Top Tips for Volunteers

Want to increase the size of your donor base? Look to your volunteers. If you've ever received a bequest from a volunteer you didn't know had means, you know what I'm talking about. Volunteers are your most loyal constituency.

Set a Google alert for each of your donors and volunteers. When you see that they've accomplished something important, recognize them!

Don't think of your volunteers as "second-class citizens." It's time to realize that volunteers are an extremely important part of any charitable organization.

Donors can be volunteers and volunteers can be donors. Let's change the way we work with everyone and anyone who is inspired by the work we do and let's stop needing them to stay in their "assigned" categories. **Both** are significant partners of your nonprofit. Recognize that many people are both volunteers and donors at the same time.

Want to engage younger donors? Many studies show that **younger donors** (millennials, Gen Z, etc.) **are much more likely to give to an organization they trust,** and they "check out" the organizations they're interested in by volunteering before giving.

CHAPTER 8

RECURRING GIFTS

What Works for Amazon and Netflix Will Work for You

Personally, I'm a recurring (monthly) donor to a handful of nonprofits, and it gives me an ongoing sense of joy and satisfaction every month when I see the donation on my credit card statement. And yet, my interaction with these organizations is typically nil. (I don't count the credit card receipt as an "interaction," sorry.)

Despite that, I continue giving and still feel good about it—probably because I can see (via their mass emails and website) the organization thriving. But what happens if and when I notice (online and in emails) a lack of growth—or change in direction—at the organization? Now the credit card statements don't make me feel so good—in fact, they uncomfortably remind me that the organization might be one that I no longer want to support. If I've had minimal or zero interaction with the organization during my years of monthly giving, I'm likely to stop the donation and move on. Let's talk about one of the greatest missed opportunities in the nonprofit world—monthly donors—and how to attract and keep these loyal supporters.

In this chapter, we'll cover:

- Your monthly donor program (or lack thereof) doesn't add up
- The biggest missed opportunity in the nonprofit world
- Why you should pay more attention to your regular monthly donors
- Regularly acknowledge your monthly donors
- Strengthening relationships in challenging times
- How to know when your donors would prefer to give

When 12 x $100 Does Not Equal $1,200

As most of my regular readers know, I'm passionate about recurring giving. As a donor, monthly giving makes me feel connected to a given nonprofit throughout the year, knowing (via monthly credit card receipts) I'm helping to sustain that organization regardless of the time of year or a particular program. For the NPO, my monthly donation is consistent, reliable, and doesn't turn on or off when there are changes or challenges throughout the year. (Every organization—for profit or nonprofit—has challenges throughout the year, and if they tell you otherwise, they're lying.)

I find myself continually perplexed at the reluctance to think of recurring donors as a critical piece of any nonprofit's fundraising program. Let's look at the math. Just a few months ago, Nonprofit Tech for Good[1] summarized the 2021 Open Data Project's findings that included these lovely points:

1. Of the nearly 600 nonprofits queried, 38% actively implement a year-round retention strategy for online donors.
2. Only 32% send an automatic "Welcome" series to new online donors via email.
3. Only 23% follow up on expired credit cards for recurring/monthly donors via email.

What the heck, right? Yes, I know, I know. The reason for the above statistics is because nonprofits are understaffed, under resourced, and they must choose where to put their time and energy. And when a donor "only" contributes $100/month, we look at that as a $100 donor. A $100 donor gets classified into the common "under $1,000" category, and the resources attached to that donor category typically include lower-level staff, less attention, and sadly, a relegation into a group of less important "givers" so that the focus can be on major donors.

This, in my opinion, is faulty thinking. Look at the three bullets above. All of those issues can be solved by simple automation. None require any significant use of resources. Still, it happens.

And here's where the math comes in. A $100 donor is a $100 donor and can be put into that "under $1,000" category. However, a $100 monthly donor is a $1,200/year donor and should be put into the "over $1,000" category. But they're not!

Let's look at retention rates too. For first-time donors, the retention rate is only about 18%—meaning only a small number of them donate again the next year—while the retention rate for monthly donors is well over 50% (Donor Perfect says 90%).[2] These monthly donors are showing loyalty to your organization, and they are far more likely to keep those monthly donations coming long-term (simply by not canceling them) than any other type of donor.

Simply put, a $100 donor is a great donor to have, and that donor, like any other donor, should be thanked, appreciated, and respected. A $100/month donor, though, should be treated like gold, or at the very least like a $1,200/year donor. Think about it, and do the math.

If You've Fallen in a Forest, Does Anyone Notice?
Build a clean and user-centric website.
Use technology to track gifts and send receipts.
Target millennials.

Yes, and . . . recurring donations are, in my opinion, one of the biggest missed opportunities in the nonprofit world. And yet, many organizations see these giving programs as their lowest priority. It's common for organizations with recurring donor programs (sometimes known as "sustainer" programs) to consign recurring donors—who may give as little as $5 per month—to their most junior staff, or worse yet, give them no staff support at all. Hmmm.

Here's one of many reasons why that's not a wise move. Consider the stats: recurring (monthly) donors give 440% more to a charity over their lifetime than one-time donors. The average lifetime financial return from a recurring donor is approximately $800, compared with a return of approximately $150 from a one-time donor. Add that to the anecdotal evidence that recurring monthly donors are also likely to give an additional one-time gift to the organization when they learn about a particular need. I'm one of those donors, and believe me, engagement matters.

Nonprofit Tech for Good[3] says that only 9% of recurring gift donors are acknowledged after month three. Yet many of those donors keep on giving. I had given gifts of various sizes to an NPO for more than four years, and I had supported them via one-time donations as well as monthly gifts. So when I canceled my recurring gift, I was pretty certain I'd get a call or email from the organization asking how they could get me back "on board."

Guess what happened? **Nothing**. It's been months and months and I've heard nothing. In fact, I finally did get an email from one of the organization's staff just last week saying that they were restructuring and would love my support—but it was clear that they had no idea my monthly gift had ceased. Did they even know that I had made those monthly gifts in the first place? Was that so much of a *transaction* to them that they didn't even feel the need to share the information with their staff? Yet I kept allowing that credit card to be charged, month after month.

The moral of the story? Notice your donors. Notice your volunteers. They're all part of the community that your organization is at the center of, and it's not right to ignore them.

How do you do it right? Here's one example. My colleague Gisèle Goldwater-Feldman, Director of Community Philanthropy at UCLA Hillel, is very clear about the importance of noticing and engaging with monthly donors. She considers it a requirement. At Hillel, the recurring donor program consists mostly of monthly donors— and they typically "sign up" when they are graduating seniors. They are referred to as their "Monthly Menschics."[4] Gisèle has created a recurring giving promotion where anyone who signs up to give $100/year or $10/month gets a T-shirt. She sent "swag" to her monthly donors to engage them during the darkest moments of the COVID pandemic. She's adamant that recurring donors get the message that they are needed and appreciated. In her words, "I want you to know we notice you."

According to Network for Good,[5] "monthly giving programs have higher retention rates that get stronger over time." How wonderful is that? Many of us know that new donors' retention rates (donors that give a first time and then give the following year) are at about 18%. Retention rates for monthly giving programs, however, ". . . typically enjoy retention rates over 80% after one year and 95% after five years."

Gisèle and her department have it right. A receipt has nothing to do with a relationship. These monthly donors have made a long-term commitment to your organization. Don't they deserve regular acknowledgment? Don't you have some swag in your closet you could send to your monthly donors to say, "I notice you and I appreciate you"?

A Really Lame Way to Lose a Donor

I get emails daily from nonprofits looking for money. Sometimes they're super professional, interesting, appealing—and even thought-provoking—but often they're none of those. When I give, they're some version of grateful, and if I stop giving, they (strongly) try to persuade me to donate again. Until, one day, when I received an email from a large university informing me that I was done giving. How can that be, you ask? Here's the story:

A couple of years ago, I signed up for a recurring monthly donation to one of my alma maters. Like most recurring donations, I let it continue and didn't think about it. As you likely know, that makes me highly valuable to the organization, because (a) it's predictable revenue, and (b) I don't need to be solicited to keep donating (at least at that level). For many online businesses, and for some offline businesses as well, recurring revenue is the gold standard. So why in the world would they tell me I was done giving?

I had lost my credit card in a movie theater. I got a new one in the mail two days later, just like the original one, but with the last few numbers changed. Although I updated the card with Amazon and my dry cleaner, I didn't go through every single transaction of the past year-plus—rather, I decided to wait until the less regular vendors noticed that the credit card didn't work, and when they contacted me to say so, I would just give them the updated card number. Pretty simple, right?

For this university development department, not so much. The email they sent said, in a very terse tone, that my credit card was declined and that I was now removed from their database. If I wanted, I could go onto their website (or call them) and start a new account, but my account was now closed. A link to the donor website was provided, but instead of linking to a section where I could "update my payment method" (standard procedure for just about every site I've ever seen), I was linked to a generic "donate now" website. Yup—my previous account was closed. I had no access to my payment history, no ability to give a new credit card—nothing.

To add insult to injury, when I shared this email with a friend who has worked for years in development, she pointed out that instead of the expected "we value you as a donor and want to make this easy for you," I got a terse email message that was akin to the "you bounced a check and are now persona non grata."

I was so disappointed. How, with all the money spent on the development infrastructure at a major university, can this happen? Is it possible the powers that be in the organization's development department aren't aware that the average recurring donor gives 42%[6] more in one year than donors who give one-time gifts? Or that the costs of maintaining recurring donors is far less than for annual givers? Or that recurring donations can provide much-needed revenue in the off-peak months of a nonprofit's fundraising cycle? Or, just as importantly, that recurring donors are more loyal and easier to retain? It will be interesting to see if they notice I'm gone . . .

Top Tips for Recurring Giving

Do you think that recurring donors are great because you can "set and forget" them? Think again. The method a donor uses to donate to your organization shouldn't determine how you treat them. Donors are human beings and not ATMs. Think about it.

When sending direct mail solicitations, offer recurring gifts first—followed by one-time gifts. Recurring gifts are MUCH more sticky, and there's absolutely no reason not to ask for both.

Typically, we only discuss multiyear gifts with major donors. Why not suggest the same to all donors?

A receipt has nothing to do with a relationship. Monthly donors have made a long-term commitment to your organization. Don't they deserve regular acknowledgment? How about sending them a "swag" or a special email "to our loyal monthly sustainers"?

A $100/month donor should be treated like gold, or, at the very least, like a $1,200/year donor. Think about it, and do the math. Research shows that monthly donors become even more committed to giving to your organization over time, showing that their value is much higher than their monthly gift.

CHAPTER 9

MANY TYPES OF GIVING

Let Me Count the Ways

A few years ago, I was on a call with the fundraising committee of a board I was on; we were going over the details of our big annual luncheon. We expected about six hundred guests. I had purchased a table, invited several friends, and was looking forward to the event. As we reviewed the "run of show" (the timetable for the event), we got to the part where the pitch for donations would be made for the guests. It was then that something very strange happened.

I heard the following: "This is the moment when everyone will pull out their checkbooks."

Let's not only look at what's wrong with that statement; let's also examine some odd practices nonprofits accept as the norm and explore how to remove obstacles to giving and maximize your existing donations by automating your process.

In this chapter, we'll cover:

- What credit cards do you accept?
- Don't rely on this payment method
- The problem with only accepting checks
- Ditch the idea of automobile donations

Do You Take Diners Club?

In 1950, the first credit card, the Diners Club[1] card, was created. It was touted as a card that could be accepted "everywhere"—or at least at any participating store.

For most of us, Diners Club cards went the way of the Rolodex and the Selectric typewriter—maybe still used by some, but not so much. For nonprofits, accepting a Diners Club card has not been an option for decades.

Depending on the circumstance, most organizations will accept cash, but not all. Because of COVID or other concerns, many major businesses stopped taking cash (e.g., Whole Foods, Sweetgreen, most airlines, and many restaurants). Obviously, cash has its issues beyond COVID (like the PTA event I once went to where the committee head was putting the cash received in her pocket "for safekeeping").

Most organizations take "all major credit cards," but they will not take "all credit cards." Whether it's American Express, VISA, MasterCard, Discover, or even Diners Club, it's important to be clear about what you accept.

Many, if not most, nonprofits really, really prefer checks so they don't have to pay the credit card fee. I've had lengthy discussions with nonprofit managers about the pros and cons of accepting credit cards as they often lament the 3% charge to do so. They often suggest strongly pushing payment by check to avoid that fee. Pushing payment by check has all sorts of issues as well. Checks can bounce. People can say "the check's in the mail." Snail mail might not make it to its destination. And most people no longer use checkbooks.

Online bill pay is great, and usually works out fine. But not all donors are comfortable with that, and it doesn't work well with immediate, on-the-fly solicitation programs. For events, asking only for checks will leave out the majority of folks who don't bring checkbooks with them. However, asking only for online payments (e.g., Square, Stripe) makes some people uncomfortable, and then there's that pesky fee.

Venmo is great, but not great for tracking tax-deductible payments. PayPal generally has a fee associated with it. And now we have cryptocurrency in all its forms. If you're thinking "Oy vey! This is a fraught issue," you're correct. And here's another wrinkle . . .

Why is it that so many solicitations from nonprofits—whether they're on the website or via snail mail—say that you can contribute by donating your car or securities?

For many charities, I think they're only saying that because someone else had it on their materials and it sounded good. My experience is that this car/securities thing has rarely been thought through.

Let's start with the car donation thing. First, I have spoken to many heads of nonprofits, and when I asked them if they really accept cars, they looked at me with a bit of a blank stare. When I finally got someone to answer the question, I was told "there are services that do that for us." None of them had ever— even once—had someone ask to donate a car—yet this "offer" appeared on their solicitations. And guess what? The truth is that donating your car to a charity is often "the least cost-effective way to give to a charity,"[2] Stephanie Kalivas, an analyst with CharityWatch, states in a CNBC article.

As to the securities thing, I myself have donated securities to nonprofits, but it's always been a challenge unless I've donated via a donor-advised fund. With more than one organization, I had to speak with the CFO and explain to them how to accept my stock. On at least one occasion, I had to walk the CFO through the process of setting up an account with a brokerage house in order for them to be able to accept the securities I wanted to donate. Perhaps the nonprofit should figure out how and if they can really accept said securities before they promote it as a means of making a donation.

Bottom line: accept that there are pros and cons with pretty much all forms of payment. Spend some time thinking about which types of payment you will accept from donors, and then create a specific, detailed plan to accept those forms of payment. Saying, "Hmmm . . . I need to get back to you on that" is not an acceptable response to a donor call.

And don't say you accept "all credit cards" if it's not true. (If you really do accept Diners Club, go right ahead.)

Cash, Check, or . . . ?

In the opening of this chapter, I told you about the event I was looking forward to until I heard these words: "This is the moment when everyone will pull out their checkbooks."

Honestly, I couldn't believe my ears. I thought I had been beamed to somewhere in *The Twilight Zone*. Checkbooks? Really? I spoke up and said, "I won't have a checkbook, and nobody I've invited will have one with them either." I was then told—in no uncertain terms—that I was wrong, and that everyone other than me and my guests would be bringing their checkbooks to the event.

Instead of just being appalled, I regrouped with, "Well, you'll have someone able to process credit card payments near the tables, right?" No.

I was dumbfounded. How can this be? The Gap and Whole Foods stopped taking checks in 2013 and 2014 respectively, and many other large retailers have followed suit. Some large chains have gone way beyond that and have even become cashless (which has its own set of problems). In the world of charitable fundraising, why wouldn't we accept as many forms of payment as our donors might want to use to donate to us? A June 2019 study by the Federal Reserve Bank[3] reports that only 6% of all payments were made by check in 2018, and that number goes down to 3% for people aged 44 and under.

Although checks are still required for some government services, certain small businesses, and some landlords, even these entities offer non-check alternatives most of the time (e.g., Venmo and the like, debit cards, or cash). Most people have some sort of checking account, but very few would carry a checkbook with them to an event.

That's not to say that checks shouldn't be accepted—but the days of referring to them as the primary, or sole, payment vehicle should have long passed. With so many options available, why wouldn't every nonprofit offer as many ways to donate as they can?

I get invitations to charity events all the time, and many still suggest I should "send my check" to their address. For me, and most people I interact with, that phrase is cringeworthy. Not only do we not pay with checks, but we also don't "send" funds other than digitally, except in rare cases (some government reason, generally). If you only accept checks or suggest that checks are the only way you accept donations, you are likely to lose a donor. Think about this: have you ever been to a department store, ready to purchase something, and you can't find a staff person to check you out? Or you don't want to wait in line to pay? You're likely to think twice about making that purchase.

When we're talking about a charitable contribution, we must make it as "frictionless" as possible for the prospective donor to contribute. In all types of sales—or when compelling someone to act—standard practice is to eliminate obstacles, one by one, to get to a "yes." The form of payment should never be an obstacle.

I was at a lunch one day, having a discussion with the development person for a small nonprofit, and we arrived at this issue. Although her site had a link for paying online via credit card, she acknowledged that the link was buried deep in the site and was therefore not easily accessible. Why? What's the thought process behind not having a donation link front and center on every single charity's website? I've heard the "I don't want to pay credit card fees" comment, but that's just archaic, in my opinion. I read "I don't want to pay credit card fees" as "I don't want to raise as much money as I possibly can for my organization."

Think about how you pay for things in your personal life. Chances are you don't pay for most things with a check. Most of your donors don't either.

Unsolicited Advice About Unsolicited Gifts

Have you ever given someone a gift "just because"? Most people have and most, if not all, would agree that it feels great to do so. More specifically, have you ever sent a donation to a nonprofit that hasn't solicited you?

I have, and it feels great to give someone (or an organization) a gift they didn't see coming. I thought it was strange, though, that when I gave those unsolicited donations, I was either questioned or ignored by the organization. It seemed like they were genuinely confused. One of them emailed me and asked who I was, how I found the organization, and why I decided to give. It didn't feel like a "get to know you better" communication—it felt more like an interrogation.

Until I researched this a bit more, I thought I was part of a minuscule percentage of donors who give money without being formally asked. But then I found some research suggesting that I'm not such a rare bird. For example, the 2019 Burk Donor Survey[4] found that 75% of the study's 12,000 (highly educated) donors reported that "some or all" of their charitable gifts in 2018 had been unsolicited, meaning they were not a result of a direct appeal or solicitation. Now I feel like I'm in good company.

So I looked for more research and found that, aside from the above report, unsolicited donations just aren't studied so much. I'm guessing the reason is that "unsolicited" can also mean "uncontrollable," and if you can't control, you can't plan, and so on. The study suggests that a significant portion of charitable giving is driven by donors' personal interests, connections, and motivations, rather than by direct appeals or solicitations from organizations.

I believe those unsolicited donations were also driven by great marketing and communication. **This includes a professional and compelling (and functional) website, great storytelling, and messaging that inspires trust and confidence in the donor.** Without all that, donors will look elsewhere. For me, if you don't have all the pieces on the above list, I'd rather give to a smaller, newer nonprofit that does have them. Also, the larger and more established the organization is, the higher my expectation is that the organization will have a professional website and a compelling, succinct story showing impact.

The upshot is that your overall and (hopefully) fully integrated marketing and communications strategies all influence a donor's giving (or not giving.) Make sure it's all done right. And finally, if you receive an unsolicited donation, consider it your lucky day—or a day where your astute and strategic marketing, combined with a bit of luck, maybe—paid off. Don't forget to thank that donor!

Top Tips for Types of Giving

If you talk about "bringing back a check" when you or your colleagues go to a pitch, think about that word "check." Does your website even allow for donations by check?

When and why would you use a check to make a donation? It's true that there are transaction fees that you don't incur by receiving checks. There are clear benefits and risks to using either checks or credit cards. Do you use a checkbook regularly? Or at all? Remember, you're a donor too, and if you don't use a checkbook regularly, chances are good that many of your donors don't either.

Let's think of a different statement than "going to meet with a donor and come back with a check." That's a transactional (read: non-relational) statement, and the check part is archaic.

Unsolicited gifts should be a cause for celebration, not a curiosity. You promote giving in public ways, and receiving an unsolicited gift means that was successful!

No friction. We must make it as "frictionless" as possible for the prospective donor to contribute. In all types of sales, standard practice is to eliminate obstacles, one by one, to get to a "yes." The form of payment should never be an obstacle.

CHAPTER 10

WHAT IS A DAF?

Understanding a Donor-Advised Fund

My family hosted a fundraiser for Sharsheret,[1] a peer-support organization to help women diagnosed with breast cancer. We've hosted many events for nonprofits over the years, and we receive invitations to buy tickets or sponsorships for nonprofits' events regularly. Of the hundreds of solicitations I've previously received, none of them—until now, with Sharsheret—have listed "donor-advised fund" as one of the ways you can donate to them. On this particular invitation/payment card, not only was it listed, but it was listed just like cash, check (ha!), or credit card—instead of being relegated to the side in tiny type (i.e., "If you'd like to use an alternative form of payment, such as a donor-advised fund, call xxx-xxx-xxxx").

As a longtime supporter and contributor to donor-advised funds, I wanted to stand up and cheer. Finally! It only took over 200 billion dollars sitting in DAFs (in the US alone) for a fundraiser to take note that maybe, just maybe, the person they were soliciting might have a bunch of money in a DAF, which they could easily use to contribute to the organization. Why has it taken this long? Let's look at DAFs, what they are, why they may or may not be effective, and how to make it easier for donors to direct these funds to your organization.

In this chapter, we'll cover:

- What is a DAF?
- Why are DAFs so mysterious?
- Who are DAFs good for?
- Drawbacks of DAFs
- How to get more DAF donations
- Make it easy for donors to pay with DAFs
- Important lessons for nonprofits receiving DAF funds
- When it's good to ask for a check

$234 Billion Opportunity—Demystifying DAFs

Recently, I've noticed that the nonprofit space is vexed by three ominous letters: DAF. We have to discuss and demystify donor-advised funds. What are they, and why are nonprofit leaders, fundraisers, and donors so wary of them? Here's a concise explanation of a donor-advised fund and why someone would want to open one. Author and NYU Professor of Philanthropy Jason Franklin writes in *Nonprofit Quarterly* (July 25, 2020 issue) that "donor-advised funds are essentially charitable savings accounts, which enable a donor to make a single contribution and receive an immediate tax credit on the gift, distributing smaller grants from that pool over time to a range of nonprofits."

Donors like them because they enable immediate tax deductions without dictating a timeframe or specific organization for donation. Nonprofits should understand and like them because they are growing like wildfire—DAFs have over $234 billion in them today, and they resulted in $35 billion in contributions to nonprofits in 2021 in the United States alone.

But even with those staggering numbers, the nonprofit sphere retains a strong distrust of DAFs. A social media post I saw summed it up: "I hate DAFs and I accept that they're here to stay." To be fair, I understand the nonprofit world's frustration. The balances in these funds are kept private, the names of many of the contributors ("advisors") are often withheld, and the amount of money in them at any given time isn't accessible. Neither is information on which organizations the "advisor" has given to via their DAF. As a board member, advisor, and donor, I am certainly acquainted with the frustration of the unknowns DAFs present— they leave nonprofits in the dark when they're trying to reach out to potential donors. To fundraisers, DAFs represent a big, mysterious, unapproachable pot of gold.

There are many steps fundraisers can take to work with DAF donors. The problem is, however, that fundraisers are so daunted by the opacity of these funds that they've thrown in the towel on trying.

Anyone on the fundraising side should work to better understand a donor's motivation for using DAFs. They are great for someone interested in donating money but not yet sure where to contribute. DAFs are great for people with appreciated stock, or people who have experienced a recent windfall, like an annual bonus—anyone who wants to put a chunk of money into an account, get a tax deduction, and not feel rushed to decide which charity to give to.

I'll add another reason for someone to have a DAF—they're incredibly easy to use. Their online tools allow you to make gifts from a computer or phone in minutes and give you instant visibility on the gifts you've given. My DAF allows me the flexibility to give to nonprofits whenever I feel like it. Another wonderful benefit is that they streamline tax reporting, saving me the end-of-year tax panic and making for a much more peaceful holiday break with my family.

Of course, DAFs are not without their drawbacks. One of the biggest negatives (one that has even Congress concerned) is that there is no minimum amount that must be forwarded to nonprofits once money is deposited into the fund—nor is there a required timeframe by which it needs to be donated. For foundations, a minimum of 5% is required to be granted out annually, but that requirement doesn't exist for the DAFs of individual donors. Some have called this "warehousing" money and claimed that DAFs are an instrument for those more interested in a tax deduction than putting their money to charitable use. In fact, in 2021, philanthropist John Arnold claimed that 10% of DAF holders made zero distributions in the past four years—a time when much of the world was in crisis. However, this isn't the norm. About 20% of DAF funds make their way to charities every year.

Having said that, Congress and various state legislatures have been trying to pass legislation that would require DAF holders to distribute their funds within a specified period of time, and even at a specific minimum amount. I support this. I think having parameters around the timeframe in which DAF money goes into nonprofit hands is important. And I think most DAF holders would agree.

I have a bit more trepidation about public calls to make the identities of DAF donors public. Making their names public would create a list of high-priority targets for fundraising teams. The floodgates would open and outreach to DAF donors would be unceasing, causing irritation that could make donors turn away from giving entirely.

It's critical that today's fundraisers understand how DAFs work in relation to their organization's fundraising strategy. DAFs are becoming more common every day. Recent reduction of fees and the elimination of minimum deposits by some donor-advised fund programs have made DAFs an option for a much larger segment of the population. (Growfund and Fidelity Charitable are two examples of these.)

So whether you're a fundraiser, donor, or board member, do yourself and your organization a favor. Learn as much as you can about how DAFs actually operate and you'll quickly realize that they are a terrific tool with minimal downsides. For fundraisers and board members, welcoming DAFs can dramatically boost your nonprofit's revenue generation efforts. For donors, DAFs are a great way to give strategically and to track your giving. Remember, they're here to stay.

Donor-Advised Funds—What Nonprofits Need to Know

Remember the fundraiser for Sharsheret I mentioned at the beginning of this chapter, and how the organization included DAF donations on their payment card? Fundraisers out there—don't ignore the DAFs. These are a big deal. Are you ignoring them because you don't know what they are? Do yourself a favor. Learn what they are. It's not rocket science. Teach every single person in your organization what they are. Make sure your board knows, too. This is a HUGE amount of money to be ignoring.

Having said that, it's not easy to know who the "owners" (advisors) of this money are and how much money is in those accounts. The institution now owns those funds, and they have no obligation to tell you (or anyone) who the money is being advised by. However, in addition to the suggestion above, here are some more:

1. You keep data on your donors, right? Ask every one of them, as a matter of course, if they have a donor-advised fund. That information alone gives you some important insight into that donor, which you can use to make them more comfortable relating to your organization.
2. Include the option to pay via a DAF in all of your solicitations for money. Show in all your marketing materials that you recognize DAFs and are happy to work with them—and that you know how they work and what their rules are (this is an important point).

3. Look at the checks you receive. Recently, a friend (a board member of a charity I donated to) called to thank me for a gift, but also to inquire about that "other name" on the check—the name of the organization that my DAF was housed at. There are many choices of institutions to house your DAF, and which one the donor chooses will tell you a lot about that person.

4. If you know someone who has just come into a lot of money or is about to, let them know about donor-advised funds. You might be surprised how many wealthy people are still writing multiple checks to charities. They are likely to be very grateful to you for introducing them to a much more efficient, streamlined, and cost-effective way to make their charitable donations. That gratitude is likely to make them more attached to you and your organization, as sharing the information shows that you really care about helping that person with their giving overall (not just for your organization).

5. If you can afford it, open a DAF yourself to experience firsthand how they work. In mine, I make contributions (technically, I recommend them) from my iPhone when I'm sitting with a fundraiser. I get a confirmation immediately, which I can share with the fundraiser while we're still having a conversation. The minimum contribution to open an account may be less than you think.

I hope that's helpful; I look forward to the day when more of that DAF money is flowing to worthwhile charities!

A DAF Donation with a Surprise

As many of you know from reading my previous book, I have set up donor-advised fund accounts for all my children. For my younger kids, the checks come from my children's (named) fund that's under my stewardship. A few times a year, I remind the kids to think of a nonprofit to support if they haven't yet allocated the funds in their account. (I "refill" their accounts annually.)

During COVID, I realized my kids still had funds in their accounts, and I told them they needed to think of a grantee to give the money to that was related in some way to the pandemic. Imagine my surprise when my son immediately told me he had an organization in mind.

Previously, I had noticed that he had about a dozen computers running in his closet—most of them obsolete or made of old parts. They ran all the time, and they were generating so much heat that we needed to move them to another part of the house. When I asked him what they were for, he told me they were processing information to find a cure for COVID. He told me that people all over the world were doing this kind of work in a form of distributed computing directed by the "Folding@home" project. He added that he was "pretty sure" the project/organization was a 501(c)(3), thereby making it eligible for a donation from his DAF.

I was a bit flabbergasted—as well as slightly intimidated by the tech side of this—but I checked online and found out that the "Folding@home" project was a twenty-year-old "citizen science" project that had been founded at Stanford by chemistry professor Dr. Vijay Pande. The project, with a tiny budget, is organized as a consortium of scientists at prominent universities. Today, there are over four million computers simulating protein dynamics in their downtime to develop new therapies for many diseases, including COVID-19, Alzheimer's, cancer, and others. Anyone with a PC and electricity can participate—even when they're sleeping!

My son and I requested a check from his DAF account, and off went $1,000 to the attention of Greg Bowman, Pande's protégé and the current director of Folding@home, now based at Washington University, St. Louis. There was an address on the website, so I was able to have the check sent without any communication with the organization.

And then Greg Bowman contacted me through Twitter. Evidently, the check went to the development office at WashU, and Greg was informed that an unsolicited donation had arrived. They also told him that one of the names on the check was that of a "known" donor named Lisa Greer and that maybe he should connect with me. Greg didn't know what a DAF was, but he's a researcher, so he did some research. Here's how he tells it:

After a VERY quick Google search, I discovered your Twitter profile and website about Philanthropy 451. From there I found your book, which I purchased immediately and started reading since it directly addressed my desire to get a grasp on how the fundraising world works (or doesn't, as I've now learned). After enjoying the first chapter of your book, I decided to DM you a thank-you note on Twitter to establish some connection, in the hopes that you'd be up for answering questions and brainstorming as I read more.

I was delighted when you responded to my DM, and even more so when you took the initiative to suggest a meeting. I certainly enjoyed the chat we had afterward! I'm still working on some of the ideas we discussed, and it would be fun to chat more about them sometime. I had assumed based on your family's giving history and the information from your website and book that you were the one who made the gift to Folding@home. On the call, I was delighted to learn that your son Jack was actually an enthusiastic member of our community who was contributing computing power and also made the gift from his DAF.

Fortune had it that our conversation also turned up another point of connection. I've been wanting to send some sort of meaningful thank you to all the people who have helped Folding@home and me during the pandemic. I had the idea of 3D printing protein structures from our simulations, but all I know about 3D printing is that it exists :) So, my ears perked up when someone mentioned that Jack is a 3D-printing guru. I followed up with a thank-you note and, since Jack is a minor, asked permission to engage with him about 3D printing.

Jack has proved to be a great mentor! In addition to printing a model for me to see how things look, he helped me find a great printer within my price range and troubleshoot some of my newbie issues, and pointed me toward some of the more advanced techniques that may be useful. I'm sure I'll have more questions for him. And we'll see if I can get the prints to go fast enough and look good enough to send to a bunch of people.

Very cool, right? (Greg left out the part that Jack is super high on the points scale for hours contributed. Mom's so proud!)

Lessons learned?

1. If you receive a check from a donor-advised fund, follow up on it! Greg isn't a seasoned fundraiser, but he was curious about the person who sent the check, did a few minutes of research online, found me, and we've developed an authentic and productive relationship. Even if they're checks from past donations, follow up on every single one.

2. Make sure there's information on your website with the address to send donations to. Don't force a prospective donor to make a call or wait for a response to an email—make it easy for them to send in a donation.

3. In addition to ensuring that your mailing address is on your website, it's also a good idea to add some verbiage saying something like "DAF contributions are welcome." By doing so, you acknowledge that you're aware of the billions of charitable dollars awaiting distribution.

The $234 Billion Mistake

Sometimes it's the little things that make your day.

A couple years ago on Giving Tuesday, I received a number of solicitations, but one in particular caught my eye. In the payment section there was a special box for "I'd like to pay by check." Woo-hoo! Am I excited because I can now pay my donation via check? Yes, but no, not really. As Paul Harvey would say, "Here's the rest of the story."

Donor-advised funds pay grants by check. Most email and snail mail solicitations ask for credit cards—only. See the disconnect?

I called my friend Noga Brenner Samia who heads up the organization that I got the solicitation from—Hillel Israel. Noga was pleased that I had noticed the box for paying by check, and she told me that she had insisted that it be on the form. Did she want the box there for people like me who might want to "put a check in the mail?" No—she wanted the box there for people like me who have donor-advised funds. (And yes, some people still write checks, but we've talked about that earlier in the book.)

Here's the point (if you haven't gotten it already): donor-advised funds keep growing and growing, and solicitations don't reflect that this pile of money is sitting there. If you make your gifts via your donor-advised fund and you read one of those solicitations, there's always a moment where you say, "Hmmm . . . I'd like to donate to this cause, but do I really want to call or email them to let them know I'm going to make my donation via my DAF?" Why should I have to do that?

Why isn't there a place where I can write (typically online, on a form) that I'm happy to donate and it will be via my DAF, and the address pops up saying where the check should be sent? Why, when my kids wanted to be part of a "donate-today-and-get-a-stuffed-animal" promotion with a wildlife protection charity, did I have to make multiple calls, be sent to voicemail, and wait for a conversation just to make the required contribution? (Just to add to the fun, I still didn't get the stuffed animal(s) after the check was sent in by the DAF, so I had to call multiple times after that.) You get the picture.

Here's a recommendation. Teach everyone on your staff what a DAF is. Then have them try to think like a donor who gives via their donor-advised fund. Walk through your pitch, your collateral, and your conversations, and notice where the pitch (written or otherwise) doesn't speak to DAF clients. Then fix it. Don't make—or continue making—a $234 billion mistake.

Top Tips for DAFs

$234 billion of charitable funds in DAFs can't be ignored. Not clear on how a DAF works? Now there are "free" and no-minimum DAF programs that you can sign up for to fully understand them. If every nonprofit staff member used a DAF themselves just one time, NPOs would embrace this method and they would raise more money overall.

Rework your promotional materials to include "We welcome DAF donations" and the mailing address for DAF payments. With $234 billion sitting in DAFs today, there's no reason to require a donor to email or call your office to give; jumping through hoops to give is a sure way to lose the donor's attention and interest.

If you receive a check or online payment from a donor-advised fund, follow up on it! Do a few minutes of research online and work to develop an authentic and productive relationship with the donor. Even if they're checks from past donations, follow up on every single one.

Trying to access some of the nearly $234 billion in DAF funds? DAF Widget is a great (and free) way to connect with DAF donors.

One more way to care about your donors. If you know someone who has just come into a lot of money, or is about to, let them know about donor-advised funds. You might be surprised how many wealthy people are still writing multiple individual checks to charities.

IT'S A TEAM SPORT

CHAPTER 11

NONPROFIT MANAGEMENT

Sometimes, You Have to Buck the System—and Now Is That Time

As someone with extensive experience in both the philanthropy and tech sectors, I believe two things to be true. First, by and large, modern nonprofit fundraising methods are archaic, flailing, and ineffective, and they often discourage new donors from giving. Second, technology can be fantastic, but technology alone cannot and will not deliver the changes the philanthropic sector sorely needs.

As a colleague of mine likes to say, "Technology is easy—it's people who are hard." Sure, he's a chief technology officer, but he also knows an essential truth. He knows that advances in technology will not solve or compensate for a dearth of human intangibles—like empathy, active listening, gratitude, honesty, and authenticity. From websites to well-being, tech tools to time wasted pandering to difficult donors, let's look at improved ways to manage your nonprofit that will welcome, instead of turn off, prospective and current donors.

In this chapter, we'll cover:

- What your website says about your organization
- How to make it easier for a donor to get their money to you
- Website mistakes and how to fix them
- Unreasonable donor demands
- Recurring donors give more per year
- The cost of losing and replacing a fundraiser
- How to help fundraisers enjoy their work more
- What's the secret sauce?
- Why it's important to merge technology with human qualities
- An effective use of surveys
- How to use technology to serve both nonprofit and donor

How to Spot a Dysfunctional Organization (Without a Single Conversation)

When I was working in the digital media/web space years ago, we had a saying that you could spot how dysfunctional an organization was by looking at its website. Sadly, that statement remains true today. When I see a website that isn't cohesive, intuitive, professional, and clear in its messaging, I'll click away pretty quickly. But I don't just leave the site.

I immediately think of the long and unproductive meetings that the "powers that be" (board included) must have had—and when they finally allowed their new site to be launched, the result was a "meh," watered-down website that doesn't reflect well on the organization and its mission. That's where the organization's dysfunctionality starts to appear.

There is a wonderful article about this by Ilma Ibrisevic on the Donorbox blog.[1] It highlights a number of important points about websites vis-à-vis donors.

Here are a few:

1. Today's online donors expect smooth, sleek, and efficient websites.
2. Per a survey by Target Analytics, **47% of donors surveyed were turned off by website usability problems.**
3. The time it takes an average user to make a judgment on your website is **50 milliseconds.**
4. Users are making assumptions about your nonprofit, how credible it is, whether they trust you enough to give you their money, whether they want to volunteer with you, and so on.
5. **Only 3% of charities rate their board and executive leadership as being digitally savvy.**

I'm not sure if point two or point five is more disturbing. So, what makes a website poor enough that users flee from it? A recent survey from Storyblok[2] tells us that "60% of consumers say they abandon purchases due to poor user experience on websites."

As a donor, I completely agree. You can't disconnect the website from the nonprofit—the website *is* the representation of your nonprofit. If your board and executive leadership tell you differently (because only 3% of your board and executive leadership are digitally savvy, perhaps?), you need to make changes to your board and/or executive leadership.

Before I talk about website design and construction, I first need to address the one thing that trumps all other issues with nonprofit websites:

Did you know that according to the 2021 Nonprofit Digital Marketing Benchmark Report by M+R, the average online donation completion rate across all nonprofits was 21%? This means that 79% of donors who started the donation process did not complete it. You must make it easy for a donor to get their money to you. While the "frictionless" discussion is concerned with experience and emotion vs. quick "in and out," the fact remains that the **execution** of the transaction must be seamless, simple, intuitive, and quick.

Once you've made the online-transaction piece simple and customer-oriented (Venmo or Zelle, anyone?), you're not out of the woods. Chances are that consumers still won't return to your website or your company because of some of the things included in Tema Frank's article on the Mirasee blog called "42 Ways to Scare Off Your Customers With Bad Website Design."[3] Hopefully, you haven't made all of the forty-two mistakes, but this list can be very helpful and enlightening. (Note that "customers" can apply to different business sectors, but the points are absolutely relevant to nonprofits.)

Still, since **trust** is one of the top reasons for donors to give or not give to a nonprofit, you can send a donor fleeing—in seconds or milliseconds—because your website isn't up to current standards of usability and professionalism.

Personally, when looking at nonprofit organizations' websites, I often see many (if not most) of the mistakes that are listed in the "42 Ways" article. Misspellings in particular make me absolutely crazy. For the nonprofit sector, there are also issues with websites that turn me (and I'm sure other donors) off from giving. These include:

1. Having to go through multiple pages to find the donation page, and then finding it difficult to navigate. Very often only credit card payments are offered, and since I typically use my DAF, I get stuck and

eventually give up. (This would likely be the same issue for people who want to send checks.)

2. Having to fill out loads of information that doesn't seem relevant—the best practice would be to require only information that is absolutely necessary to put through the donation. (These "required" fields should be clearly marked—usually with a red asterisk—so I can get through the form quickly.)

3. Not showing a clear way to contact someone at the NPO if I have a question. Often an email or phone number is given, but rarely of someone who would actually respond in a timely manner.

4. Messiness. Make sure that your links work. If you have a page or section that isn't quite complete, it's okay to write "this section is under construction" or "this section coming soon." It's not okay to have a title with the "lorem ipsum" copy filling the space.

5. Not including an immediate thank-you pop-up that tells me why my donation is important. Many NPOs make these pop-ups all about my tax-deductible donation, but at this point, I'm not donating because of tax deductibility. I'm usually giving because something about the organization (and what it does) is compelling and has likely emotionally moved me. The tax piece is fine, but shouldn't be front and center on that initial acknowledgment/communication.

6. When going to an organization's website (when I'm giving for the first time), I want to know who the leadership is (ideally with linked bios of them), how the organization started, where they're located, who they serve, and what their accomplishments have been. Knowing where my money's likely to go (what the funds will likely support) is ideal. Note that operational costs, in my opinion, should be included in that as I want to know that the organization has the resources to pay their staff a living wage (or better) and keep their business going. The last thing I want to glean from a website is that the nonprofit's operations don't seem to be able to support its mission.

7. Another piece that's important—and that I look for—is the opportunity to become a monthly/sustaining donor. If that piece isn't clearly

offered in the "donate" section, that tells me that they aren't up to date on how people give and they have no problem leaving potential donations on the table. It also connotes that they are likely to be like the board members and executive leadership who aren't even reasonably tech savvy. In other words, leaving out the options for monthly giving and multiple methods of giving (there are many—including DAF gifts) tells me that this organization is stuck in the mud and won't be successful. I'll happily give my money elsewhere.

A final note—once I see a poorly done website, I will remember that organization's name and brand long-term. I might tell my friends about it, too. In other words, there are lasting implications—not just the air of dysfunction—of having a lousy, poorly constructed website. Having some cute videos on TikTok won't help.

Donors: When (and Why) to Just Say No

It's a story that most fundraisers are familiar with: major donors make demands and you and your team lose your minds trying to retain the donor's money while keeping "on mission." If you have ever felt that a donor "stole" hours and hours of your time that you'll never get back, this next part is for you.

Town and Country magazine, the publication that, as their website tells us, showcases "a world of exceptional people and exclusive places," published a telling article about "high-maintenance donors." They provide some shocking statistics on difficult donors vis-à-vis fundraisers. They report that:

- 66% of fundraisers surveyed report that **donors have used controlling behavior that compromises the mission of the organization.**
- The fundraisers they surveyed report that donors have implied or stated outright that **they would not make a gift unless they got what they wanted.**
- 77% of fundraisers surveyed say that they have worked with donors who have "**used their influence for favors or benefits they don't de-**

serve." (The "deserve" part there is annoyingly subjective, but you get the picture.)[4]

Based on my experience, here are some examples of unreasonable donor demands:

1. A donor insists that an academic institution allow him to "weigh in" on decisions about the organization's leadership and curriculum.

2. A (married) donor demands an out-of-town date with an unmarried staff member, and the organization tries to "keep him happy" by insisting that the staff member comply.

3. A donor offers to give a "large" gift for the nonprofit to install a garden on their premises. Fair enough—but they also dictate that the money be spent immediately and that they should be included in a press release honoring them for that gift. We later find out that the donor had some legal trouble and wanted to use their "charitable support" to, well, secure a "get-out-of-jail-free" card.

4. A board member insists that "all gifts are fungible" and ignores the restrictions on several endowment gifts.

5. A donor requires that the fundraiser (or, most often, the executive director) attend events with them—often out of town. The donor doesn't seem concerned about the costs to support that requirement, including travel costs, opportunity costs (costs of being out of the office focused on one person), and personal costs (time away from home and family). Note that this is not to secure a larger gift— rather, it's a requirement (implicit or explicit) of the donation.

Know that this isn't an exhaustive list as most readers will have had their own experiences with unreasonable donor demands. (Feel free to send me your stories!) The point of all of this is that these are ridiculous and obnoxious requirements from donors who use their "gift" as a carrot. Some people enjoy watching staff scurry around doing things to make them happy. It's a control thing. Don't give them the satisfaction.

The message here is that every hour you spend with, or relative to, these types of donors is, most often, a colossal waste of time. This "pandering" takes away time and energy that could be used to further your organization—and it often has no impact on the size of the "gift."

So how do we know when jumping—when they say "jump"—is worth it and will result in a substantial donation? The time we spend wringing our hands and analyzing these situations could be better used elsewhere. Even if one out of every ten of these donors gives a giant gift, it's still, in my opinion, rarely worth it. The exceptions to this are (a) if you're truly certain that the time spent will result in a specific gift, and/or (b) if not doing what the donor wants will likely impact other donors' gifts.

There are definitely some gray areas and some unknowns there, but I would start by saying "no" to anything that seems or feels out of line. Despite what some people think, donors won't mind being told "no." It gives them clear boundaries, and if they are entranced by what your organization does, they'll understand that they hit the boundary and they'll happily give, especially if you back that up with a specific reason. Some good reasons would be "that's inappropriate" or "that's unethical" or "doing that would distract us from our mission."

I recognize that this can feel difficult and a bit scary. So here's a **mantra** or two for you as you contemplate saying "no" to a donor. Read and repeat: "**There are over 600 thousand millennial millionaires out there who we aren't soliciting while we waste time on this one person.**"

Remember: only 9% of recurring gift donors are acknowledged after month three. **Recurring donors give 42% more money per year[5] than one-time givers.** Overall, recurring revenue from monthly giving is now 22% of all online giving[6] and grew over 16% in 2021 over 2020. They are also more likely to give a second gift during the year. **Why aren't we allocating more resources to monthly giving?** Oh, I remember—it's because we're spending so much time with an unpleasant, hard-to-please donor.

By spending so much time and so many resources keeping a comparatively small (and often homogeneous) group of donors happy, we are not only shooting ourselves in the foot, we're leaving huge amounts of money on the table.

We *must* learn to think differently about the donors we approach. As I mentioned previously, the Great Wealth Transfer—the twenty-five-year period that will see the largest wealth transfer in history (some say $63 trillion)—began about three years ago. That money, or much of it, is going to the younger generations—from Gen X to Gen Z (with the millennials in between)—and women in those age categories and older will also see a great influx of money. It's estimated that **by 2030**, more than two-thirds of wealth in the US will be held by women[7]. It's true that today, baby boomers still hold most of the wealth, but that's changing daily. As of late 2022, **approximately 1.79 million of the 22 million millionaires in the US are under thirty.** Yet many, many nonprofits are still prioritizing older men in their fundraising. It's critical that we look at these numbers and realize we can't wait another day to learn about what these other demographic groups want and expect when it comes to charitable donations.

Think of the hours and hours you've spent trying to keep one cranky donor, when you could have spent that time learning about and communicating with younger donors and women.

Somewhere between 60% and 85% of today's HNW (High Net Worth) individuals are self-made, yet many or most of them aren't anywhere on your radar. **We can't waste another minute before we learn about and embrace these folks**. We need to find the time and resources to create and build relationships with people who are not the usual suspects, and we need to do it now. The days of only focusing on the "regulars on the list" who have long-term inherited wealth are ending, as only about 20% of wealthy people today (at least in the US) inherited their money. The idea that thirty-year-olds and women neither have nor control money hasn't been true for years.

Philanthropy Revolution details a number of negative personal experiences I had as a "newly wealthy" woman. It's painful to realize that every day others are going through what I went through. So think about the true value (both short- and long-term) of every minute you spend with your donors. You might want to make a change.

How Not to Lose a Good Fundraiser

According to the National Council of Nonprofits, "most charitable nonprofits rely upon the generosity of donors for some or all of their funding. Consequently, fundraising is an activity of major importance to the charitable nonprofit community."[8]

I think that's an understatement. Simply put, the vast majority of nonprofits —whether they be a "one-person-shop" or a huge institution—rely on charitable giving for their existence. Since about 80%[9] of charitable giving overall comes from individuals (as opposed to foundations, government, and corporate grants), the person, or people, who interacts with individual donors is a critical member of the nonprofit's team. So we treat those fundraisers accordingly, right? Unfortunately not.

Various research tells us that between 50% and 75% of all nonprofit fundraisers are, in any given year, considering leaving their jobs. A 2019 report in the *Chronicle of Philanthropy*[10] shows that about 30% of fundraisers plan to not only *leave* their jobs, but their intention is to leave the sector completely. Let's not forget that without funding—largely brought in by fundraisers—nonprofits cannot stay solvent. This is a critical problem.

So why is this happening? It seems counterintuitive, since most fundraisers say that they strongly believe in their organization's mission. In fact, many left the for-profit world to be able to work in a job that feels more purposeful. However, in the US Bureau of Labor Statistics[11] survey, the summary shows that nonprofits (in general) pay fundraisers low salaries, require no "experience in a related occupation," and don't provide on-the-job training. Not so compelling.

Fundraiser Seth Rosen wrote a wonderful (but painful) piece on Joan Garry's blog called "How to Avoid Burnout."[12] The story tells how Seth found himself in the emergency room with severe medical issues that came from the stress and intensity that he lived through as part of his fundraising job. Thankfully, Seth is okay, but it seems clear that nonprofits need to support and protect their fundraisers much more than they do now.

If fundraisers are the lifeblood of a nonprofit—if fundraisers have a direct impact on whether the organization succeeds in its mission—then why do we treat them like automatons? I'm not suggesting that there aren't many wonderful organizations that do treat their fundraisers like gold, but the ones that do are in the minority.

In the *Chronicle of Philanthropy* 2019 report, they note that of the 1,035 fundraisers queried, "78% said they wished they had more time to spend meeting with supporters."

Yet I hear story after story about NPOs telling their fundraisers to use scripts word for word. I hear about larger organizations telling fundraisers to stay "in their lane" and just to "bring back a check." Many nonprofits have a very short window for a fundraiser to be successful—and that window doesn't often align with the creation and cultivation of an authentic relationship.

So what's a nonprofit leader to do? Here are a few tips to keep a good fundraiser:

- Pay your fundraiser(s) a competitive salary (and look to the entire sector for comparison information).
- Think of your fundraiser(s) as an educated, experienced professional and treat them accordingly. (Telling them to "make sure to bring your client/donor list from your last job so that you can bring in some money pronto" is the opposite of what you should do.)
- Make sure your fundraisers are working in a supportive environment and that they have all the tools they need to help them be successful. If they'd prefer to work at least some days from home, let them. Having a professional staff member sit at a desk just to "keep an eye on them" isn't okay.
- Make sure your senior fundraisers are part of your executive team. Fundraisers are the catalyst for bringing money into your NPO, but fundraising is everyone's responsibility. A good fundraiser can't do their job effectively if they don't have information about what's happening at their organization. Withholding information about an organization from fundraisers is like shooting yourself in the foot. Remember, donors want to hear about successes and challenges, so the fundraisers must have this information.

- Provide professional development to not only the fundraisers, but also to other staff and to your board. Everyone at the organization needs to understand best practices in nonprofit fundraising—they need to understand that this work is hard, takes time, and can be extremely successful given the right environment.

- Reward donations that come from patient, ongoing, focused relationship building. Recurring gifts should be acknowledged as a "win." One-time transactional gifts are great in the short-term, but not so great in the long term.

- Possibly the most important tip is to make certain that your organizational culture has zero-tolerance for condescension, belittling, or yelling. Yes, this includes donors—regardless of how much money they give.

Since that "Great Resignation" of 2021 doesn't seem to be slowing, we need to do better than our sector is doing now. Continuing to push the "transactional" way of fundraising will keep those fundraisers walking out the door, and nobody will benefit.

When Well-Being and Fundraising Are Aligned

Fundraising is hard work, and as I mentioned above, fundraisers burn out at an incredibly high rate. According to studies, we know that fundraisers stay at their jobs on average for sixteen to eighteen months, depending on which research you access. We've also seen studies that report as many as 51% of fundraisers say that they plan to leave their job within two years, and of those, 30% report that they will likely leave the sector altogether.

Clearly, that research includes fundraisers at all levels, including development professionals who are still learning the profession. However, some of those surveyed are longer-term, higher-level, often major gift-specific fundraisers—and it's estimated that **the cost of losing and replacing a staff person in those categories can be as high as 500% of their annual cost.** Grenzebach, Glier, and Associates' article, "Calculating the Cost of Losing High-Performance Fundraisers,"[13] walks you through the thought process you should employ when you're thinking about the "care and feeding" of your longer-term, higher-performing fundraisers. You'll see that the cost of losing good fundraisers can be devastating to a nonprofit.

So, what to do? If we can't increase their compensation package, there's not much we can do, right? Isn't turnover just an assumed risk of any nonprofit? **Not so much.**

What if we could help fundraisers enjoy their work more by changing our methodology a bit? What if we added some "secret sauce" to the mix? What if that secret sauce could alter the emotional reaction both fundraisers and donors get when they've been involved in an "ask," turning it into a "feel-good" experience for both parties?

Let's first look at the donor/volunteer side. As I wrote in "Feelin' Groovy" in Chapter 1, the answer lies in years of research into the benefits of volunteering and giving. Both volunteering and giving (or either one) provide myriad emotional and psychological benefits to the volunteer or donor, and, simply said, they create happiness. Happier people—especially when their happiness was facilitated by your nonprofit—are more loyal, more concerned about the health of your organization, and therefore more likely to donate (and donate again).

So instead of thinking of fundraising as transactional, think of it as providing happiness. For anyone who has been impacted by or is connected to your nonprofit or your cause, a non-transactional engagement with you is likely to create or enhance a long-term connection—and help these "fans" of your cause become happier.

I'm aware that many fundraisers are taught to think about the happiness they facilitate for donors. Whether as a reminder or new information, it's important that all fundraisers understand this connection between the facilitation of a gift and the donor's happiness and well-being. But here's the point: **fundraisers deserve feelings of happiness and well-being too.**

Nonprofits work hard to stay on mission, and most work like crazy to keep donors on board. It's unusual, though, to find an NPO that sees their fundraisers as equally important. That needs to change. With the rate of fundraisers leaving their jobs (or the field entirely) only getting worse, we need to do all we can to ensure that fundraising is both professionally gratifying and personally satisfying for the fundraisers.

For the moment, let's focus on the fundraisers themselves. **If this profession isn't providing personal satisfaction and gratification to these key employees, the health and sustainability of our sector will be at great risk**. This doesn't include the obvious impact on revenue, nor does it account for the loss of fundraiser/donor relationships, which can be even more detrimental. We can't afford to ignore the impact of good fundraisers leaving. So how do we change the recipe for successful, sustainable nonprofit fundraising to include an emphasis on long-term retention of our fundraisers? **We add the secret sauce**.

Take a look at the *Yours for Business* article called "Emotions in the Workplace."[14] It confirms how happiness, joy, pride, and feeling valued are all critical emotions that most people need to stay in a job. When a fundraiser is trying to convey to a donor that giving is good for their personal well-being, it would be great if the fundraiser believes that for themselves. In the fundraiser's case, the "giving" is the giving of themselves to their organization's cause.

Expanding the usual "fundraiser-facilitates-joy-for-the-donor" paradigm by adding the secret sauce (the fundraiser's emotional benefit) just might help to right our sector's boat. This way of thinking will make the new "recipe" one in which three elements are present:

1. The Organization, with its important mission that helps to solve a problem
2. The Donor, who is looking for purpose, personal satisfaction, and joy in giving
3. The Fundraiser, who is putting their passion, soul, and time into work that gives them happiness, joy, pride, and a sense of value

So the next time we're talking about the emotional and psychological benefits to a volunteer or donor, let's add fundraiser to that conversation. If fundraising feels like a grind—and lacks a sense of emotional well-being—how can a fundraiser, even if they choose to stay at the NPO, authentically communicate all the good things that come with giving?

Why Fundraising Teams Can't Let New Tech Tools Obscure Meaningful Donor Relationships

It bears repeating: no matter what shiny new tech toys your team is working with, empathy, active listening, gratitude, honesty, and authenticity are the essential drivers and indicators of future success in fundraising. The future of philanthropy lies in fundraisers successfully merging these pivotal human attributes with key advances in technology.

Why? Because donors want to be seen as individuals. We don't want to be thought of as a piggy bank or an ATM. We hate pandering and game-playing by people who seem to just want our money and don't care about us as human beings. When an authentic connection is made, we feel noticed as a real person with our own interests, desires, and needs—not as a caricature of a person with money. It will be much easier to procure a gift from us if we feel like we have an authentic relationship with the person and the organization we're thinking of supporting. (In fact, many donors, including myself, have given several unsolicited gifts just because we feel a connection to the organization.) New technological tools ease the cost of scaling and segmenting donor outreach, but often this comes at the cost of personalized contact. New technologies must be implemented within the context of authentic, meaningful relationships.

Let's start with two examples of often minimized but completely essential duties of any fundraising team: surveys and list management. There are myriad programs and tools that can make both of these tasks more efficient and less resource-heavy—as long as this technology is used effectively by fundraisers.

On surveys: my friend Elad Dvash-Banks runs development for IKAR, a renowned, cutting-edge religious community in Los Angeles. When COVID hit, IKAR took its programming online and experienced global growth in interest and viewership. When about 500 people outside the United States not only tuned into their High Holiday programming but also donated, Elad wondered how best to engage these folks further. With in-person meetings out of the question, I suggested Elad query these new donors via a quick and easy online survey to ask them about themselves and to best understand what they desired in their relationship with the organization.

The results? The survey got a 70% response rate, with many respondents expressing appreciation that the organization even cared about their opinion and surprised that the survey had not been accompanied by a request for money. The donors responded with the ideas, suggestions, and thoughts that mark a nourishing donor-fundraiser relationship. Some even provided unprompted donations in response to the survey. Elad made the best of technology available to him by combining it with an honest, donor-specific approach that aligned with his organization's values. Simply put, Elad thought like a human being and donor partner, and the result was spectacular.

Applying a similar ethos to list management will set your organization apart immediately. This is an area that nonprofit organizations want to (and should) use internally to help their organizations improve their "moves management" systems. For completely different reasons, this is an area that donors wish nonprofits would address.

There is no greater example than Giving Tuesday. Sure, Giving Tuesday is terrific, as it raises hundreds of millions for nonprofits every year. However, it also makes many donors want to throw their computers or phones out the nearest window. Every year, I wonder why I must get a barrage of impersonal and increasingly desperate emails from every organization that has ever received my email address—emails that ignore previous gifts or disregard giving criteria I've already expressed. Some come hourly throughout the day. (In 2022, one prominent, established NPO emailed me fourteen times on Giving Tuesday.)

That type of marketing and communication is just about guaranteed to make a donor feel that an organization views them as a "checkbook" rather than as a person, or that the information they've provided has been ignored. The message is that they are just another cell on a spreadsheet.

When I've discussed this frustration with nonprofit leaders—and even with other donors—I've received mixed responses. Some tell me that this type of list segmentation is too resource-heavy and that I should just "suck it up" on Giving Tuesday. Maybe.

But here's the concern. Even if I could personally just brush off my frustration with mass Giving Tuesday solicitations, many donors won't. In fact, you can bet that for many donors, receiving four to six increasingly desperate-sounding emails will cause them to develop a very negative association with that nonprofit, and they will never consider giving to them (regardless of the organization's impact).

So, what to do? Use technology to create substantive, highly personalized, informed databases that have a focus not only on money and capacity but also include meaningful and personalized information about who these prospects are as individual human beings. Many in the NPO world are aware that major change is necessary, but inertia and fear can get in the way. As I wrote in *Philanthropy Revolution*, ". . . innovation and change are inherently uncertain. But it's high time we did this differently and started teaching it differently too. There are so many development professionals out there who can't wait to deliver substantial change to the sector."

Improvements in tools like surveys and list management (many including cutting-edge AI) are just the beginning of what we'll see in this new era of philanthropy and fundraising. When we enrich new tech with human authenticity, personalization, empathy, and active listening, we will have created a more productive, efficient, and compelling version of the nonprofit sector. The positive effect this will have on our organizations' respective missions will be breathtaking.

So, when you are considering purchasing new tech tools for your nonprofit, ask yourself and your board: "How do we take this tool and apply our humanity to it?" This is how we create the fundraising utopia we need. Let's do it together.[15]

Top Tips for Nonprofit Management

Don't make someone have to log on to your website to give. Why not make it as easy as possible for them to send you money?

Look at your staff churn rate. If your organization has a pattern of frequent staff turnover, make it an imperative to figure out why and how that will impact your donors. Donors don't love having to recreate the relationship with a fundraiser over and over again. If your donor's "relationship manager" leaves, don't just assign them another—reach out to the donor and learn what will work best for them. This "outreach" should be done by someone on your staff who the donor knows, if possible.

Are you doing your work a certain way because, once upon a time, a particular donor demanded it? Making poor decisions because of a single donor isn't good business practice. You know that, right?

Examine all the different steps of your fundraising effort. Isolate them, and ask yourself (or your team) if there's a reason they need to be done the way you're doing them. If nobody knows the reason, forget the "because-it's-always-been-that-way" answer. Can that step be done differently? Can your process be changed to adapt to the present time? Hard questions, but it will be worthwhile to ask them—even if you don't make changes right now.

When you are considering purchasing new tech tools for your nonprofit, ask yourself and your board: "How do we take this tool and apply our goals, mission, and humanity to it?" Tech tools that are purchased only because they're new and shiny won't serve you well.

CHAPTER 12

BOARDS AND BOARD MEMBERS

The Status of Your Board Will Make or Break Your Fundraising

While serving as board president of a nonprofit organization, I was once yelled at during a formal board meeting. A longtime board member stood up, pointed his finger at me, and accused me of "just wanting to change everything" (that status quo is sometimes hard to buck). This inappropriate board member behavior seems to pop up often, unfortunately. Here's another example: a friend of mine told me about a board member pouring water on the head of the organization's executive director because he objected to changes in the status quo. Clearly these people need some kindness, consideration, and care. However, they might not need to be on the board anymore.

I've served on lots of boards and, as those who have read *Philanthropy Revolution* know, that experience hasn't always been the most fulfilling, successful, enjoyable, or productive (regardless of the mission of the particular organization). In fact, many of those experiences were the epitome of frustrating. Why?

Let's break down the reasons a board may be weak or unhealthy and share ways to improve the functioning of your board. Along with answering the "why" above, I'll be answering additional questions, because the health of your organization just may be tied up in the "who." Whether you're just getting started or going through an overhaul, ensure your nonprofit is built on a strong, healthy, and engaged board.

In this chapter, we'll cover:

- The duties of a board (they're more diverse than you think)
- Tough questions to ask yourself about who is on your board
- What makes a successful board
- What might be weakening your board
- When it's best not to serve on a board
- How to build a better board

- Who should be on your board
- How thinking younger will improve your board and your organization

Does Your Board Need an Intervention?

For me, several of the boards I've served on seem to see the board as a "necessary evil." (Some might say boards are "a pain in the neck.") Many senior staff see their boards as having only three functions:

1. To fund the organization's overhead and work.
2. To ensure that the organization is in legal compliance with nonprofit rules and regulations.
3. To hire, evaluate, and set the compensation of the executive director.

That's not a full description, though, of what a nonprofit board does. If it was, my guess is that far fewer people would want to sit on boards. Like me, many board members want to get their hands dirty (in a good way!). The National Council of Nonprofits defines board members as:

> ... the fiduciaries who steer the organization toward a sustainable future by adopting sound, ethical, and legal governance and financial management policies, as well as by making sure the nonprofit has adequate resources to advance its mission.[1]

Now that sounds more fulfilling! Their definition goes on to include how board members play important roles in shaping the culture of a nonprofit, along with being ambassadors of the organization. If your board members aren't doing the above, then your nonprofit organization is missing out on a valuable (and essential) tool. Ask yourself these questions:

1. Do you have legacy board members who don't benefit the organization, but who you keep on the board because you don't want to hurt their feelings?

2. Are you bringing board members on solely because of their financial contributions, without regard for their ability to provide guidance and strategic help, and to serve as an ambassador and advocate for your nonprofit?

3. Does the adage "we do it that way because that's what we've always done" sound familiar? If so, your organization's reluctance to change—to develop and sustain a strong, diverse, effective, engaging, responsible, and strategic board—is doing a disservice to your constituents, supporters, and anyone who has a stake in your organization's long-term success.

I know that every nonprofit is doing its best to impact its constituents and mission. However, this is not a new problem. Fundamental and substantive changes to boards have not happened much in decades. Consider this: based on a survey of nearly 1,000 directors of nonprofit organizations, the 2015 "Survey on Board of Directors of Nonprofit Organizations"[2] found that 27% of respondents don't think their boards have a strong understanding of the organization's mission and strategy; 65% don't think their fellow board members are very experienced; and about half don't think their colleagues are very engaged in their work (48%) or fully understand their obligations as directors (47%). The report adds, "Our research finds that, unfortunately, too often board members lack the skill set, the depth of knowledge, and the engagement required to help their organizations succeed."

Hmmm. "Skill set, depth of knowledge, and engagement" are required. I don't see "big bucks" listed there. I do agree that board members should all contribute to the organization's fundraising efforts, but that contribution doesn't necessarily have to be directly asking your friends and colleagues for money. There are many ways that a board member can help in fundraising—and ensuring the organization's financial stability—that doesn't feel uncomfortable or onerous. Look at the bigger picture!

The Taproot Foundation recently published a great primer for what a successful/functional board of directors looks like called "4 Qualities of an Effective

Nonprofit Board."[3] While I recommend reading the full article, the four qualities are:

1. Experienced in critical service areas.
2. Focused on governance and advising, not day-to-day tasks.
3. Diverse in backgrounds and skills.
4. Comfortable raising resources—financial or otherwise.

If the areas that the piece discusses sound foreign to you and not at all similar to your current board, then you need to start making changes right away. The health of your nonprofit depends on it.

There is no shortage of articles and studies dealing with this issue. In addition to the resources listed above, check out BoardSource (always my initial go-to), the *Stanford Social Innovation Review* (SSIR) reports, any of the established philanthropy periodicals, and even sector-specific pieces like "Effective governance: the roles and responsibilities of board members"[4] (it deals specifically with the healthcare field, but most of it applies to any NPO).

Building a Better Board

In *Philanthropy Revolution*, I include a chapter on boards that's called "What Money Can't Buy: Trust, Good Governance, and Better Boards." In it, I note that "more than once, I have walked away from charitable organizations for reasons of principle. I've done it even when I believed in the good work they were doing."

Why walk away when I believed in the work? The list of reasons is, unfortunately, quite long. Suffice it to say that it had a lot to do with issues around governance, leadership, best practices, respect, and trust. The hesitance on the part of several board members to participate in any type of giving or fundraising was disturbing as well.

Shouldn't it be obvious that leaders of a nonprofit—knowing that nonprofits live or die based on funds raised—need to have an active part in fundraising? I understand that many board members bring expertise, connections, and resources, and many are very uncomfortable asking others for money. I say that as long as you have a diversified board—some members who are comfortable asking for money and others who aren't—that's just fine. However, a board member who won't even make an email introduction to a prospective donor or who doesn't see themselves as an ambassador for the organization shouldn't have a board seat.

In short, don't ask or agree to serve on a board if:

- You don't really believe in (or maybe even understand) the nonprofit's mission.
- You're just doing so to "make friends."
- You don't see it as a privilege to serve.
- You don't feel comfortable telling others about the organization's goals and its good work.
- You're allergic to change.
- You don't see yourself as part of the solution to the growth and sustainability of the organization.

The *Harvard Business Review* published a wonderful article on this about twenty-five years ago entitled "The New Work of the Nonprofit Board."[5] Sadly, the article is just as timely—and the issues just as current—as they were then. In other words, not much has changed in twenty-five years.

Here's how the article begins:

> Effective governance by the board of a nonprofit organization is a **rare and unnatural act**. Only the most uncommon of nonprofit boards functions as it should by harnessing the collective efforts of accomplished individuals to advance the institution's mission and long-term welfare. A board's contribution is meant to be strategic, the joint product of talented people brought together to apply their knowledge and experience to the major challenges facing the institution.

The article's authors use the term "new work," which they define as work that "defies the conventions that have regulated board behavior in the past." Change! Innovation! How exciting is that? Change and innovation in service to strengthening a nonprofit organization for the long term, helping it to deliver greater impact than ever before? I'm in!

Anyone who's served on a nonprofit board knows that there will be board members who find this "new work" to be scary, off-putting, and maybe even threatening. One of the ways to avoid these issues is to be more careful—and, in fact, innovative—when choosing your board members. **Here are some suggestions for building a healthy, strategic, supportive, and productive board of directors:**

- **Look carefully and strategically at your board composition.** Is your board diverse? A healthy board should incorporate a diversity of backgrounds (economic, ethnic, gender, etc.), identities, knowledge, experiences, ages, and even manners of speaking. Put some extra emphasis on having folks on your board who have a strong connection to your organization's mission.

- **Make sure you have some sort of term limits.** Boards where everyone has been there for a dozen or more years can't help but have difficulty seeing the forest for the trees. Echo chambers and boards are a bad combination.

- **Make sure your board members are respectful human beings.** Screamers, bullies, and those who don't play well with others shouldn't be welcome on any nonprofit board.

- **Make sure your board members recognize the variety of people who make up your staff**—from professionals and creatives to admin people and janitors—and that they see all of them as contributors to the organization's success.

- **Make sure your board members aren't afraid of innovation or change.** A good board member will welcome innovation and change, and if they have to understand a new technology or business model, so be it.

- **Ideally, board members should not be afraid to "get their hands dirty."** A nonprofit that doesn't let its board members volunteer is missing the point.

- **Make sure you have current bylaws, accurate and up-to-date financials, and a good sense of the history of the organization** and its previous successes and failures. Board members do better when they have a sense of the culture and history of the group before they even attend their first meeting.
- **Ensure that you have a document with clear expectations for board members.** This should not only be financial, but if there is a financial requirement ("give or get" or "give and get" or otherwise), make sure it's made clear before the member joins the board. The financial requirement should be explicit, transparent, and equitable. Make sure that you're not excluding diversity in favor of money—but if someone isn't in a position to give *and* refuses to help the organization raise money, they might not be a good match for your board.

These are only suggestions (although they're based on lived experience), but this is not meant to be an exhaustive list. Different organizations require different board member attributes. However, the above is a good base on which to start building (or rebuilding) your board of directors.

As I've mentioned previously, there isn't a shortage of excellent guides, articles, and opinion pieces on nonprofit boards. Here, again, are a few examples of sources that I have found useful:

- Nonprofit Finance Fund
- BoardSource
- National Council of Nonprofits
- *Stanford Social Innovation Review*

A good, well-comprised, strategic board can ultimately make or break a nonprofit institution—and donors outside of the institution are much more likely to trust an organization with a strong, well-functioning, and innovative board of directors. Make yours count!

Why the Reluctance to Diversify Boards?

The composition of nonprofit boards, or most any governing board for that matter, is important. The people chosen to be board members set and/or reflect the culture of the organization. Or do they? And is that the goal?

If I asked a bunch of random people if they thought a board should reflect the organization as a whole (including staff, donors, volunteers, and beneficiaries), I believe they would say "of course!" And yet . . .

Reading a number of recent articles about board composition, I was struck by a quote cited in a BoardSource blog titled "Reflections on Trust and Its Relationship to Racial Inequity on Nonprofit Boards." Specifically, it referred to a statement included in a recent article in the *Stanford Social Innovation Review* (SSIR) referring to a very compelling/concerning study by Echoing Green and Bridgespan. (All of the above are well worth reading.) The quote suggested that funders, when confronted with questions about diversity and philanthropy, would likely say, "I'd like to fund solutions generated by communities of color, but they don't have sufficient evidence of effectiveness or capacity to execute."[6]

I fear that sentiment of "I'd like to . . . but" is exactly what many board members would say when asked why everyone on their board of directors looks the same. The comment above suggests that every person of color is thrown into a big basket, where there's a "they" who are all the same and who all have the same ability (or lack thereof) to be effective or to execute. I've heard this said about women and young people too.

I'm sure there are many more reasons that boards don't include or value diversity. Some of those reasons are benign and a bit lame, and other reasons are distasteful and possibly racist, sexist, misogynistic, or worse.

Let's just think practically. If you're on a board where everyone looks just like you, think about how silly that is. Do you really want everyone to just agree on everything and then go home? Is doing so at all productive or fulfilling, and does it help even one bit to promote mission success? There are plenty of research studies that show that diversity—with its inherent range of perspectives—forges innovation and, in turn, stability.

Not only are the vast majority of nonprofit boards not diverse ethnicity-wise, but they're typically homogeneous in just about every other way as well. I was once on the board of a nonprofit that focused on issues relating to girls, and imagine my surprise when I found that most of the board members were men.

I was on another board that helped kids who had life-threatening illnesses, and I still can't believe that of the more than twenty-five board members, I was the only one who had a kid who had a life-threatening illness. What's up with that?

I think there are several reasons for boards not being representative of the population they serve (or even representative of their staff and volunteers!). Here are a few:

1. Boards start off with a big donation or two—typically from older white guys (and sometimes women). The board is then constructed from friends of those original donors. Fair enough, but does that help the organization?

2. Boards start off with donations from a few folks as above, and the board is built out in a way that makes the original donors feel comfortable—and ensures that everyone at the table agrees with them. (Are you noticing that beneficiaries and mission aren't part of the discussion yet?)

3. In the pursuit to raise as much money as possible, new donors ask if their large gift can be a quid pro quo for a spot on the board. Who's going to say no? (Yes, the executive director should say no, but they report to the board. So goes it . . .)

4. Board members are asked to "give and/or get." Since everyone on the board now is the same age (generally) and from a similar background, the discussion around someone younger or of a different background will become "can they really achieve the give/get?" (This one drives me completely crazy—has anyone looked at the age of the tech gazillionaires of the last decade or two?)

5. Board development is not a big focus for most boards. The volunteer pool of a given organization should always be looked at as a resource to build out boards, but that happens, well, almost never. Volunteers and donors are often looked at as different species from one another.

6. If the board happens to realize that having a homogeneous group is a really bad idea, they still won't move forward to fix it, as they don't want to expend the resources needed to recruit (and train!) board members whose inclusion would make the board more diverse (and, by doing so, more appropriate, successful, innovative, etc.)

Stop asking why you haven't raised more money and look internally for a moment. Is your board comprised of lots of people who look the same or are of a similar age, gender, or background? Maybe consider the prospective donors out there who would like to support or join a board that includes someone who is much like them. Broadening your board is the first step to broadening your reach and, in turn, increasing the size of your pie.

Creating and nurturing a diverse board does more than increase revenue and reach. It will also help you in just about every way you can think of. Differing opinions offer different solutions. Different perspectives foster an innovation mindset. It also affords your organization the ability to have your board members—your "ambassadors," if you will—bring your message to a much wider range of people.

The only downside, if you want to call it that, is that your board members will no longer sit at a meeting absently nodding their heads in agreement at whatever is discussed and then go home, with the meeting accomplishing nothing.

We can and must do better. Our organizations, from top to bottom, are depending on us to do so.

How Many Millennial Millionaires Are on Your Board?

Do you think that your board doesn't need to include young people because they aren't big donors? Think again.

A November 2019 Coldwell Banker report[7] tells us that there were 618,000 millennial millionaires in the United States as of that time. With the current pace of people becoming millionaires in the US over the last two and a half years increasing dramatically—even in 2021 over 2020—we can expect that number to now be closer to (or exceeding) 700,000.

In fact, a recent chart from the Federal Reserve[8] tells us that US millennial wealth more than doubled since COVID started—from $4.55 trillion in Q4

2019 to $9.13 trillion by Q4 2021. If the Coldwell Banker report was updated today, it's likely that the number of US millennial millionaires is now over 1.2 million (assuming the millionaire piece of that increased at the same or a greater pace than the rest).

The CB report goes on to tell us that the average age of millennial millionaires is thirty-four, and 60–80% of all US millionaires are, as Esther Choy[9] calls them, FGWs (First-Generation Wealthy). (You might want to read that again—believing *The Great Gatsby*'s "nouveau riche/new money" are tacky and low-level appears to now be an archaic concept.)

So why is this age group almost completely ignored by nonprofit boards of directors? Why, with a push toward diversity on boards, are millennial millionaires rarely even part of the discussion about board development?

I hear the same comments over and over again about not considering millennials for a board seat. Here are the most common ones:

1. **"Millennials are slackers. They're lazy and entitled. Why would we want one (or more) on our board?"**

   Response: First, this is offensive, and why wouldn't you want them on your board? They're the future of your organization, and your board must reflect your constituencies. Saying you welcome younger people without having one or more on your board sounds insincere.

2. **"We're so forward-thinking that we have a board just for the millennials. It's called the 'Junior Board.'"** (My answer to that is always "the Kids' Table" isn't a substitute for a diversified board.)

   Response: Junior Boards may be appropriate in some instances for some young people, but they still shouldn't be a way to exclude millennials from the "Big Board."

3. **"Oh, I understand why we should have a millennial on our board of directors. It's so we can engage the young person (millennial) so that they'll go home and get their parents to give us money!"**

   Response: This answer is just offensive. No matter the board member's age, they shouldn't be thought of only as a link to another person.

4. **"What could a twenty- or thirty-year-old possibly contribute to our board?"**

    Response: Perhaps they could contribute another point of view beyond your homogeneous board makeup that likely doesn't fully represent your constituents, volunteers, or future?

5. **"Millennial-age people don't have the money to meet our giving (or give and get) requirements. We'd have to give them a special 'deal' that wouldn't be fair to the others."**

    Response: See any definition of millionaire, and note that most of the millennial millionaires have between $1 million and $2.5 million in assets. A special "deal" is suggesting their money isn't as "green" as other donors' money.

6. **"We need to focus on diversity now. We can't be bothered with this issue."**

    Response: Great news! You can have many different kinds of diversity on your board, including age diversity. You can even have, for example, a thirty-year-old woman of color!

It must be said that absolutely no group should be ignored solely on the basis of age. Regardless of resources, everyone has something to offer. Are they right for your board? Maybe, maybe not. Could they be a volunteer for your organization, and some type of donor as well? If someone is engaged with your nonprofit and your mission, deciding if you engage with them solely based on a wealth-engine profile is callous, unfair, and likely to actually damage the long-term health of your organization.

Top Tips for Boards

Is it possible to build a more generative, conscious, and productive board? Think of your board members as natural partners in the fundraising process.

Look carefully at your board composition. Do you think that young people don't have a place on a board because they aren't big donors? There are at least 618,000 millennial millionaires in the US alone. Don't put them at the kids' table.

Let's just think practically. If you're on a board where everyone looks just like you, think about how silly that is. Do you really want everyone to just agree on everything and then go home?

A good, well-comprised, strategic board can ultimately make or break a nonprofit—and donors outside of the institution are much more likely to trust an organization with a strong, well-functioning, and innovative board of directors. Make yours count!

Board members are ambassadors! Shouldn't it be obvious that these volunteer leaders of a nonprofit—knowing that nonprofits live or die based on funds raised—need to have an active part in fundraising? There are myriad ways that board members can help raise funds without doing anything that's uncomfortable for them. If they have the will, you'll (together) figure out a way to help them help your organization.

THE FUTURE IS BRIGHT

CHAPTER 13

INNOVATION

The New Era of Fundraising

What do these dates have in common: February 16, April 21, May 5, June 10...? They're all "Innovation Days" recognized in various parts of the world.

I think any day is a good day for innovation. Does innovation suggest change? Yes. Is change scary? Yes. Once you get past the scary part, is innovation gratifying? Generally, yes. Let's break it down further and look at how innovation may enhance your fundraising efforts.

In this chapter, we'll cover:

- An organization doing fundraising the right way
- A cash flow solution
- Simple changes that impact your nonprofit in a substantial way
- The Holy Grail of fundraising

Why I'm Obsessed with This Nonprofit

In early December 2022, I saw a video in my feed that captured my attention like no other. In fact, this video encapsulates, in about two and a half minutes, almost everything about the new era of fundraising that I preach about daily. First, a bit of history.

The organization that produced the video is the English National Opera (ENO) and is one of only two principal opera companies in London. With origins in the 1880s and its official start over ninety years ago, the ENO's vision, as per their website, is: **"Lives changed through opera."** Their mission statement asserts that the **"English National Opera exists for everyone, creating new experiences with opera that inspires, nurtures creativity and makes a difference."**

Like many other nonprofits, the ENO's funding comes from a variety of sources, including government grants, foundations/trusts, individuals, and companies, as well as earned income. In early November 2022, Arts Council England (ACE)[1] announced that they would **cut off 100% of their funding** to the ENO unless the organization relocated to northern England—hours from London. The ACE funding was about $15 million, which reflects about a third of the ENO's annual budget.

The ENO decided to mount an integrated, multi-channel, creative yet fierce opposition to the cuts. By November 29, they had generated a very strong response. By the end of November, the ENO had created a Change.org petition and secured over sixty thousand signatures. By late December, they had over eighty thousand signatures.

They mounted a professional, passionate, and motivating performance/protest outside of the ACE offices. But that wasn't all. This became an "all-hands-on-deck" effort, and some say it's making headway.

The ENO created a compelling video from one of their recent opera performances, and it was circulated by opera singers, staff, so-called "competitors"—such as Opera Europa and the Royal Opera House—and well-known leaders and influencers (I found it via a post by former First Lady Cherie Blair). They had staff and supporters wear T-shirts and buttons saying "#LoveENO." They garnered support and tweets/postings from government officials, international opera stars, and fans worldwide.

Since I'm not an "opera person," I can't tell you anything about the quality of the ENO's programming—but I can tell you that this organization is spot on with many of its marketing/communications efforts. Take note of these, as they offer a bit of a blueprint for other NPOs to follow:

The ENO website[2] is terrific, with a style that's clean and simple, easy to navigate and digest, and at the same time very informative. For example, the categories on their website include—with equal footprints—schedules for their season, ticket sales, giving, other means of support, special offers for diverse and/or underserved communities, etc. Since they manage the theater they use, they even give equal screen real estate to non-ENO productions!

On the front page, they have a section called "Your First Opera" for those new to opera performances. In that section, there is an informative, nonjudgmental, and non-condescending explanation of "What to expect," information on the history and highlights of their theater, dress code, opera etiquette, and links to overviews of each opera being presented. Somehow the ENO managed to present all of this—and more—in a manner that is very concise, uncrowded, and graphically easy to read (larger font, anyone?). Everything about it says, "We welcome you—come check us out!"

The "About" section is clear, well organized, and all about inclusivity. Content-wise it includes, in one simple section (with compelling and appropriate color images for each) everything from the obvious mission, vision, and history, but also professional development, funding sources, sustainability, diversity, facility rental, and even financial reports (i.e., the answer to "What's the impact of my donation?") and again, a block about supporting the organization.

In their "Discover Opera" section, they have subsections for their kids' television show (yet another channel), their past programs (including residencies, school programs, and special events), and their diversity programs, including those supporting the deaf, neurodiverse, physically challenged, cognitively impaired, etc. They even have a program called ENO Breathe for people recovering from the effects of COVID.

I've rarely seen this much information presented in one super clear website. They did one more thing that I've rarely—if ever—seen on a nonprofit's website. There's a style guide where you can easily access logos and understand how to use them. On their fundraising page they offer text donations, an answer to "Why donate now?" and an answer to "How will we use your donation?"

As many of you know, I'm a big proponent of using video messaging for fundraising—especially when videos are personalized to the recipient. In the case of the ENO, their video included messaging—both explicit and implicit—that I think everyone could learn from. On the explicit side, the song specifically tells you what you get with the ENO. In the lyrics, the singer sings about ". . . art that's radical and popular," "younger kids get in free," what your experience will be, and what will happen to the opera "with no consistent funding." It does so with humor and music. It's easy to understand every word. It talks about inclusiveness, and it shows what their performers might look like (i.e., diverse).

As to the piece's implicit messaging, it conveys serious art, but art with levity, a professional performance (the singer is quite impressive), and a need for support. However, it doesn't ask for a donation or a gift anywhere in the song. Instead, it conveys that the ENO is warm and welcoming, with interesting performances (in English) that are high-quality and compelling.

They do not say they need your money now because of a budget deadline. They don't assume you're a regular donor. They don't assume that you know anything about opera or about ENO, yet they don't exclusively speak to the newcomer audience (as opposed to the opera aficionados). They reach out to you by doing what good art does—it makes you feel and **think**.

This video made me go to their website and news articles, learn about what they do, and consider giving to them (even though I'm not an opera fan per se). Why? Because of everything I just wrote about. I love the video and its persuasive storytelling (and creativity, of course). I love that the website understands that I might be a "newbie" to opera, and all of their messaging makes it clear that a big part of the ENO's reason for being is to embrace and welcome newbies like me. In that way, I felt as if the video and website were speaking to me personally.

I also love the crystal-clear messaging in the video (and throughout the website) that explains the financial pickle they're in right now. Both the video and the website convey a sense of urgency, but not panic. Their communication overall never sounds desperate, and the website makes it clear that despite the financial issues, they're moving full steam ahead with producing programming for the coming year. In other words, there is an emotional, compelling message—never pushy—that feels completely authentic.

Finally, the ENO's overall messaging shows that they are interested in having a relationship with me as a person—not just as someone with means. I don't think that anyone could look at that video and not be personally moved. Take emotion and authenticity, mix them with professionalism, quality, and listening skills, and you have the beginning of a beautiful relationship that's mutually rewarding as well as financially productive.

Just like with friends and family, a real relationship means you care. With a nonprofit, a real relationship also means that you are invested—emotionally and otherwise—in that relationship's long-term success. ENO's messaging conveys that the relationship with them is ready when you are, and I hope we can all learn from them. Join me in wishing them success!

Four Innovative Yet Simple Ways to Help Your Nonprofit
According to a 2017 survey by SSIR,

> ... most nonprofits know that delivering the same services in the same manner is insufficient. But unfortunately, most also struggle to anticipate emerging opportunities for distinctive offerings or approaches that might extend their reach or magnify their impact. Perhaps that's not surprising. Deviating from the norm—to pursue novel principles, embrace unorthodox thinking, and learn from instructive failure—is difficult. Like their peers in the for-profit world and the public sector, it often takes a crisis for nonprofit leaders to truly break with the status quo.[3]

Hmmm ... seems like there's been a bit of a crisis recently. Have we broken with the status quo? Are we doing things differently than we did in, say, March of 2020? SSIR's study continues:

> The answer to nonprofits becoming proactive and effective at innovation lies largely in committing to a continuous, intentional approach. For most organizations, meaningful progress against the innovation-aspiration gap requires systematic exploration, experimentation, and trial and error, where learning compounds over time. Innovation is neither magic nor mystery; high-performing nonprofits demonstrate that organizations can deliberately cultivate the capacity to innovate.

There are literally hundreds of innovations that have impacted nonprofits since the pandemic began. We were doing things by trial and error during those two years—trying to keep our nonprofits in business and working hard to make sure that our programming priorities were strategic and on target. Technology helped with a lot of that—and so did government subsidies. For many, "surprise" gifts from new major donors were transformational. For others, staffing became a challenge—but in many ways, a blessing, too. For some, shared services became not only a good idea but a necessity. I dare anyone to tell me Zoom wasn't, in itself, transformational.

Happily, I'm hearing from fewer people that they can't wait to get back to "the way we did it before." Most everyone I know thinks Zoom meetings, flexible office/work-from-home environments, and hybrid galas are here to stay, and have transformed how we do our work (for the better).

To that end, I offer some of the most simple changes you can make that can impact nonprofits in a substantial and meaningful way. Without a world crisis, they might be considered radical and not worth changing the status quo—but after our recent wake-up call, they're innovative, easy to implement, and they make a difference.

1. **A cash flow solution.**

    It's no secret that most nonprofits receive as much as 30% to 50% of their annual revenue in December. Understood, but what do you do when you have more expenses than you can predict in Q2 or Q3? To help with this common dilemma, **ask your DAF donors to send their gifts between March and September instead of at the end of the year.** As you know, most DAF funds stay in their accounts for a while, and DAF account holders get no additional benefit from making their gift at year-end. As a donor, if I know that it helps your NPO by making my DAF grant in the middle of the year, I'm happy to do so.

2. **An easy-peasy way to increase your donor pool.**

    According to Neon One's Fall 2021 report[4], 79% of a nonprofit's volunteers also donate to their organization. The status quo response to this is often "Meh . . . they're small donors and they don't have the capacity to give more." Really? Do you know this to be true? Do you know each of your volunteers so well that you're aware of their bank accounts? Stop assuming and look at your volunteers as potential donors. How often have you heard of a big bequest coming in and it's from a volunteer that you didn't know had means?

3. **A way to access the money you're leaving on the table.**

    Engage younger donors—or even donors who you just don't know so well. If someone has a passion for what you do, get to know them (and that doesn't mean just by reviewing wealth-engine data). It's likely that you don't know everything about everyone you need to. Big houses and expensive cars don't mean as much as you think they do.

4. **Put your mouth where your money (and time) is.**

If you believe in an organization and its mission—whether you're a donor, staff member, volunteer, or board member, you want your resources to combine with others to help the organization be strong and successful in achieving its mission. The best way to do that is to share your passion. (Note: this is different than "asking your friends for money.") When the nonprofit you support achieves something amazing, share that info with your friends and family. Show your pride in being part of something that's meaningful and flourishing.

Maybe these seem like obvious suggestions to you, but they are absolutely not the norm for most fundraising organizations. Whether you work or volunteer for—or give to—a particular nonprofit, you can be part of positive change just by using these small "innovations."

The Holy Grail of Fundraising

Despite all data to the contrary, nonprofits just don't seem to be "getting it." For comparison purposes, let's look at the for-profit world. Recurring revenue has been the big thing in business for years. Online, recurring revenue has been one of the metrics for companies to be able to go public—or be acquired—and mint billionaires.

In the nonprofit world, recurring revenue is the Holy Grail of fundraising. Or is it? In order of importance, where do fundraisers put donors who give their credit card number to be charged monthly for, well, forever (unless they get cranky and stop)? It's clear that, in a world of "major donors" and big galas and Giving Tuesday and legacy programs, regular monthly donors rank don't rank so high on the laundry list of donor categories and programs. But they should!

Consider this:

*   Recurring (monthly) donors give 440% more to a charity over their lifetime than one-time donors. The average lifetime financial return

from a recurring donor is approximately $800, compared with approximately $150/annually from a one-time donor.

- 52% of millennials are more likely to give monthly vs. a one-time donation.

- Monthly donors continue to donate to a specific organization for much longer than other donors. In fact, after one year, 80% of monthly donors continue their giving to a particular organization, and after five years, 95% continue.

- Since many organizations take in more donations at the end of the calendar year, resource allocation is typically skewed to Q4. Recurring monthly donors, though, don't care about the end of the year—their donations come through, day in and day out, all year long.

- As more organizations develop recurring monthly donation programs, they will be able to more closely match costs to revenue. Budgets and resource allocations can be "smoothed out" by recurring monthly donations.

Knowing all this, why is it that only 9% of recurring monthly donors are acknowledged after month three? (Even a quarterly update would be nice . . .) My guess is that the nonprofits are worried that "reminding" a donor their credit card is still on file, being charged every month, will make them think twice about continuing to donate. That's like saying that getting a copy of my cable/internet bill every month will make me want to move to another provider. Hmmm . . . doesn't work that way, folks.

Another thought as to why these monthly programs aren't the "darling" of fundraising organizations is that they aren't big ticket. Tried and true, but not big individual numbers. Buildings aren't likely to be named for someone who gives $50/month for a decade. So . . . resources aren't put toward these programs.

Think about any ongoing subscriptions you have. How often do you switch it to a competitor? Almost never, for most people.

There is no reason why a monthly donation program—just like a subscription program—shouldn't be a standard part of any nonprofit's fundraising efforts. If you don't have such a program now, start it immediately. It's not so hard, and it will create a revenue stream that could help your organization in myriad ways. Millennial donors, anyone?

Top Tips for Innovation

If you haven't done so already, it's time to rethink the way you work with staff. There's evidence that staff working from home are often more productive than those working from an office. Not sure that we could have imagined that pre-COVID.

"Normal" has changed. The pandemic years have pushed us to be innovative, responsive, and resourceful. Let's keep that going!

More expenses than your nonprofit can predict in Q2 and Q3? Ask your DAF donors to send their gifts between March and September instead of at the end of the year. Get innovative!

Virtual events can be amazing and more inclusive than in-person events. Don't assume that your virtual events won't be successful—many have been more successful since the pandemic than the in-person events pre-pandemic.

For virtual events now and going forward: invite guests, speakers, and presenters whom you could never have gotten into one place if the event was live. With an online event, geography is a nonissue! Technology has opened a new world of opportunity—and that opportunity means access to a giant donor pool that was previously inaccessible.

CHAPTER 14

THE FUTURE OF FUNDRAISING

We Don't Need a Crystal Ball to See What's Coming

We are all prone to imagining utopian versions of the future—a world cured of cancer, successful against climate change, and rich with widespread happiness, health, and freedom. When we discuss how these changes will come about, the answer nearly always screams "technology!"

Like many others, the philanthropy world seems to suffer from this stilted misconception. Many who work in our sector believe that bringing new tech tools onboard will—by themselves—streamline fundraising, increase gifts, expand the donor pool, and reduce expenses. Not so fast.

Let's revisit some of the most important points of this book (spoiler alert: they involve relationships, communication, and impact). We'll take a look into the future of philanthropy, how tech may or may not be the answer we seek, and how the next generation feels about giving.

In this chapter, we'll cover:

- What donors want
- The state of giving: a few facts and stats
- The Great Wealth Transfer
- Giving 2.0: The next generation has their own interests in giving

Three New Studies You Need to Know About

The Lilly School of Philanthropy released three new study components as part of its excellent research series, "The Giving Environment."[1] The findings see the school's esteemed researchers provide a better understanding of what makes donors "tick" in today's world. These new releases specifically build on their documentation of a significant, continual drop in individual donors' charitable contributions since 2008. Thank goodness someone's paying attention—

and taking a hard look at how donors think and feel. Here's a great quote from the study, from Dr. Una Osili, Associate Dean of the school:

> Our newest findings make it unmistakably clear that donors not only want to understand the impact of their gifts but value organizations that intentionally foster meaningful relationships with their donors. While such donor expectations are not new, our research suggests donors have increasing expectations for how organizations build connections with them and communicate the scope of their impact.[2]

What follows is a summary of what they found. Their findings validate and add context to many topics we've discussed:

1. Donors want meaningful, personal connections with nonprofits, and those connections (or lack thereof) are a major factor in determining their giving. This seems to offer some proof that fundraisers would be wise to focus on authentic relationships with their donors as opposed to the much more common transactional encounters.

2. Communicating fundraising messages that evoke "a positive sense of connection" are the most effective. As "The Giving Environment" summary explains, effective communication will "induce an empathic and/or moral response without also inducing strong negative feelings of sadness or guilt." Very different from many of the solicitations that have been used for the last several decades.

3. The study also found that video was a very effective communication channel compared to other types of communication with prospective donors. In this case, "the video tested generated a 43% increase in the connection rate among its viewers." It's important to note, though, that the content and the medium of video combined to create an effective message. Video's great (I suggest it for thank-you messages to many donors), but the technology alone won't do the trick.

4. Donors want to understand the impact of a nonprofit's work. As the report states, ". . . a message that shows the impact of a nonprofit's

work draws people in and causes them to want to connect. Importantly, showing the impact was also effective for people who indicated that
they had not made a donation to any charitable cause in the last 12
months."

5.   Different people often respond differently to the same message. In
these studies, age and gender made a big difference relative to donor
responses. It's important to note this and to use this finding to test
(ideally formally) your fundraising solicitation's messages. In addition, noting that even after taking into account age, gender, and other
factors, individuals can still differ in their reception to messaging—
because they're individuals.

If you're not already a subscriber to the Lilly School's wonderful and helpful
publications, do check them out.

Gazing into the Immediate Future of Fundraising

The article below was featured in the September issue of *ZGive* magazine. I
think they do a good job covering the nonprofit sector—they consistently present compelling perspectives.

On July 1, 2022, the cover of the highly regarded thirty-five-year-old
publication *The Chronicle of Philanthropy* read "**The Giving Crisis—How
Fundraising Can Bring Americans Back to Charity—If It Changes.**"
Despite previous issues of this and other publications talking about "storm
clouds ahead" or "future-proofing," this cover created alarm in the community.
It's the first time I've seen something this strong—an image and statement that
drives home the message that change in the philanthropy sector is critical. Specifically, change in the way nonprofits raise funds must happen now.

When I wrote *Philanthropy Revolution*, I encountered a large number of
young, mid-level fundraisers and nonprofit leaders who told me they were well
aware that wholesale change was necessary in the nonprofit world, but they
didn't feel there was a "safe" forum to voice this need—nor the ability to make
change, given their current positions. Some of the more senior fundraisers, on
the other hand, were incredulous that I would even use the term "revolution."

They claimed that all was fine in the way they operated and that it was the fault of the donors that they didn't give as much as they should, or at all. A few claimed that fundraising challenges and the need for change only existed for the "smaller" organizations, and that the legacy, institutional nonprofits were doing everything correctly. After all, if those organizations had existed for decades, they must be doing something correctly, right? Wrong.

Here are some data points to prove that *The Chronicle of Philanthropy's* cover was accurate:

1. Despite a massive increase in new donors during COVID, the number of new donors in 2021 essentially remained flat.

2. 82% of eighteen- to thirty-four-year-olds who heard about Giving Tuesday 2021 participated, yet most nonprofits claim that young people "don't have money" and instead focus on donors in their forties and above.

3. 18% of Gen Z donors (currently age eleven to twenty-four) want nonprofits to ask them for donations more often and said that they would increase their gift if asked. Unfortunately, most nonprofits don't consider this group worthy of "cultivating."

4. As of late 2019 (the last year that research was released), there were 618,000 "millennial millionaires" in the United States. Yet the vast majority of nonprofit boards have zero millennial members, claiming that this age group "doesn't have the means to contribute."

5. As per *Nonprofit Quarterly*,[3] there are approximately $234 billion sitting in donor-advised funds in the US. While some of that money does go to charities every year, the total "balance" in those funds continues to increase every year. For whatever reason, most nonprofits seem to be intimidated by DAF donations, and therefore they don't make it easy for DAF donors to give.

6. Over the last several years, retention rates of new and existing donors continue to decline, with retention rates of new donors in the 18–22% range, and retention rates of existing donors in the 40–45% range. This is disturbing to almost everyone watching the stats on the issue.

7. Recurring revenue programs are one of the bright lights in the fund-raising sector, with more and more donors giving monthly. Although all ages give monthly, many more young people give monthly than their elders. However, most nonprofits don't see the benefit of focusing on this as a $50 monthly gift is put into the "bucket" of a $50 annual (or small) donor, despite monthly donors being much more "sticky" than other categories of donors, and therefore that $50 monthly donor should really be categorized, and stewarded, as a $600 annual donor. This, unfortunately, isn't happening so much.

So where are the bright lights? Happily, there are many and most of them have to do with technology. Technology continues to evolve, and the number of innovations in the "phil-tech" field are just becoming well-known now. Many of them mirror the for-profit world, but with adjustments for the nonprofit sector. Examples include:

1. Better methods, including AI, of parsing customer (and prospective customer) lists are being created.
2. Zoom and other video technologies help reduce costs, retain staff, and even allow nonprofits to send custom video thank-you messages. (This often results in increased "stickiness" and reduced costs.)
3. New and improved technologies allow donors to make a more frictionless donation. This includes giving via text message, but also giving via nontraditional means, such as DAF gifts, appreciated securities, and cryptocurrency.
4. Technologies can pull information from social media and other sources to better qualify and locate prospective donors.
5. Programs now exist that allow free and near-immediate surveys to be sent to donors, allowing a much better and personalized relationship between donor and nonprofit to evolve and thrive.

The pandemic gave many organizations an opportunity to pause and evaluate their strategies and future plans. It also allowed many entrepreneurs to have more time to solve problems and provide new and existing tools for the nonprofit community. Our challenge now is to embrace change—at all levels of the philanthropic sector—and to "carpe diem"!

It's True—More Than $9 Trillion Coming to Nonprofits

It's happening!

If you haven't heard about the Great Wealth Transfer, now's the time to learn about it because, according to the *Wall Street Journal*, the transfer has begun. Some $70 trillion will be distributed in America alone over the next twenty years according to research firm Cerulli Associates. Of that, it is estimated that about $9 trillion will go to philanthropy, with the balance going to heirs. (Some of that money going to heirs will no doubt end up in nonprofits as well).

Surprisingly, according to the *Wall Street Journal*'s article,

> . . . people aren't waiting until they die. Annual gifts taxpayers reported to the Internal Revenue Service—a fraction of the gifts that flow outside the tax system—rose to $75 billion in 2016, from an inflation-adjusted $45 billion in 2010. Over that period, the amount that people could give away without paying taxes on gifts rose from $1 million to more than $5 million for individuals, and from $2 million to more than $10 million for couples.[4]

The article points out the continued increase in gift-tax exemption to $11.7 million for individuals and $23.4 million for couples, which is scheduled to drop back to the previous $5 million individual level by 2026. The article goes on to remind us that ". . . many recipients are guided by different priorities and politics than their givers."

What does that mean for nonprofits trying to navigate this new reality? It means it's a new ball game out there, and fundraisers need to adapt. It's true that charitable-minded parents are more likely to raise charitable-minded kids, but expecting that those kids will give to the same organizations as their parents is wishful thinking. Young adult donors are much more interested in impact than their parents are, and for them, causes are more important than institutions.[5] In addition, the ability to volunteer for an organization you're interested in giving to—providing hands-on assistance to a nonprofit—is valued much more than with earlier generations. (So if you're an organization that keeps the volunteers separate from the major donors, you might want to rethink that.)

There is no shortage of information available about this "new" generation of donors, with more research coming out all the time. In a nutshell, though, it's critical to realize that the time to learn about younger donors—what makes them "tick," what's important to them, and how they're different from their parents—is right now. That doesn't mean you have to ignore your long-term supporters, but you must carve out time every day to think about how you're going to interact with the millions of young people who will receive a large sum of money from their parents in the next two decades. More than nine trillion dollars. Wow.

Eighteen percent of Gen Z donors say they would give more money more often if they were just asked. You want to raise more money? Accept that there are many donors you're not reaching. Get to know them! (Caveat—asking them in the way you've asked older donors is unlikely to work, and asking them relentlessly is likely to turn them off altogether.)

EVERYONE is a donor. Whether it's giving money, volunteering at your kid's school, or delivering food to a new mom, everyone has "given" at some time. So when soliciting for a gift, think how you would like to be approached.

Learn about younger donors. Find out what's important to the next generation as they, and you, prepare for the great wealth transfer. How can you work together for the future of fundraising?

Listen up! Create a safe space for all members of your organization to be heard. You might discover some innovative and effective ideas from unexpected sources to help your nonprofit move forward.

Embrace change—at all levels of the philanthropic sector—and "carpe diem"!

GLOSSARY OF WORDS DONORS USE
THAT YOU SHOULD KNOW

(and Words You Use That Donors Don't Know)

Philanthropy Jargon Translated

Some days, I don't get calls or emails from fundraisers or development people (it took me a year or so to realize that they were one and the same). Instead, I get calls and/or emails from "Advancement Officers," or "External Relations" people. Thinking that I'm not about to get hit up for money, I take the call . . . only to find out that these people's titles are fancy names for fundraisers and development people. (Meant to be misleading? Perhaps . . .) Although a conversation with some of those people was worthwhile, I wish I'd known the truth before I took the call.

Hoping to save you from the same "surprise," I've assembled a list of fundraising terms that are commonly used during interactions between fundraisers and donors. It's not a comprehensive list—as new terms come up all the time—but it should help remove or reduce the miscommunications that often occur between donors and fundraisers.

A GLOSSARY FOR FUNDRAISERS OF TERMS
THAT DONORS COMMONLY USE
WHEN DISCUSSING NONPROFITS AND GIVING

Bequest	Gift or donation given to a charity when the owner has passed away, per instructions in their estate plan.
Board Member	A member of any type of board (for-profit or non profit); may be a committee or an actual board of directors/trustees.
Donor-Advised Fund (DAF)	A charitable investment account sponsored and run by a financial institution or community foundation.

It's essential for people involved in nonprofits to understand what these are. More and more people are using these every day. The best solution is to open one yourself and see how it works!

Donor

A person who gives to your organization, financially or otherwise (including giving a coat to a needy person during the holidays, for example).

Estate Plan

A plan for the dissemination of a person's assets and responsibilities when they die or should they become incapacitated.

Get Involved

This may or may not relate to money. It covers any type of involvement with your organization, and financial contribution is only one of those methods of involvement.

Gift

Anything given to anyone, ideally due to kindness or gratitude, but sometimes to create a benefit to the donor.

Gift in Kind

A non-cash gift.

Impact

A strong (positive) result that financial support of a charitable organization or program has enabled. For most donors, these should be clearly quantifiable.

Legacy Gift

Money left to your organization in a donor's will.

Liquidation Event

A financial transaction where ownership and/or assets are turned into cash. For donors, this often means a sale or public offering of a business.

Major Donor	Someone who makes the largest donations to your organization or has a significant impact.
Philanthropist	Investor, contributor, or donor to a charitable organization.
Salon	A gathering of people held by a host for learning, fundraising, or both.
Support	Anything given to a nonprofit by a donor (including nonfinancial gifts or a donor's time, expertise, household items, or even signing a petition).
Trust	A legal document where property is held by one entity for the benefit of another.
Unsolicited Gifts	Donations your organization receives without asking for them.

TERMS YOU USE THAT DONORS DON'T KNOW

What Fundraisers Say:	*What Donors Hear:*
Advancement	I'm getting a promotion?
Appeal	Pitch for money, often religion-oriented.
Call to Action	Anything that makes me want to get involved.
Capital Campaign	Something to raise a lot of money. Usually relates to a building or large program.

Cultivation	What? I'm not a plant.
Development	Someone who works in fundraising, OR someone who develops programs, including for film and television.
Donor	Someone who gives something to a nonprofit.
Donor Pyramid	A pyramid showing who gives the most or the least?
Endowed Chair	I know what an endowment is, but what does a chair have to do with it?
Endowment	A long-term fund that keeps organizations going.
Engagement/Engagement Manager	Someone who throws parties?
Fundraiser (person)	Someone whose job it is to get money from me for their nonprofit.
Fundraiser (event)	An event designed to raise money for a particular organization.
Gift in Kind	Anything I want to give to a nonprofit other than money.
Giving Tuesday	A day when I want to hide because I'll get barraged with solicitations from often hundreds of organizations, all wanting my money that day (even if I just donated to them last week).

Lapsed Donor	This sounds like something religious. Or does it mean that I didn't do something you wanted me to?
Legacy Gift	A gift that will ensure my legacy. Not sure how this works.
Lunch Meeting	A way to ask me for money disguised as a "get to know you" meeting.
Major Gift	Anything that is really big. Unclear how big it has to be to be called "major."
Matching Grant	A financial gift that is doubled or tripled (matched some way) for a certain period of time. The mechanics of this aren't always clear.
NGO	Isn't this something about organizations overseas?
NPO	The medical term for "Nothing By Mouth"?
Nonprofit "Shop"	A place where donors can shop to help raise money for the organization?
Philanthropist	A donor who gives a large amount of money.
Planned Gift	A gift I plan to make in the future.
Prospect	A prospective client/partner/donor?
Quiet Period	I don't understand why you would want to keep fundraising a secret.

Recurring Donation

A gift that I give an organization on a regular basis.

Relationship Manager

What's the difference between this and a fundraiser? Couples therapist?

Restricted Gift

A gift (financial or otherwise) that has restrictions on it.

"Send in a Check"

Especially if I'm a younger donor, I might not understand "Send in" (do you mean snail mail?) or "check" (do you mean virtual, or … ?).

Support

Not necessarily money. Help of some kind: professional consulting, volunteering, offering your garage for storage, etc.

Tax-Deductible Amount

The amount of a gift that I can deduct on my taxes.

Unrestricted Gift

A donation of money that has no restrictions on it.

BIBLIOGRAPHY

Chapter 1

(1) Baghai, Pooneh, Olivia Howard, Lakshmi Prakash, and Jill Zucker. "Pooneh Baghai." *McKinsey & Company*, July 29, 2020. https://www.mckinsey.com/industries/financial-services/our-insights/women-as-the-next-wave-of-growth-in-us-wealth-management.

(2) Jacimovic, Darko. "Incredible Millionaire Statistics & Facts for 2023." *MoneyTransfers*, May 30, 2022. https://moneytransfers.com/news/2022/05/30/millionaire-statistics.

(3) "Generosityforlife." May 22, 2023. https://generosityforlife.org/.

(4) Wallace, Nicole. "Where Are My Donors?" *The Chronicle of Philanthropy*, June 5, 2018. https://www.philanthropy.com/article/where-are-my-donors/.

(5) Pew Research Center. "America's Changing Religious Landscape." *Pew Research Center's Religion & Public Life Project*, May 12, 2015. https://www.pewresearch.org/religion/2015/05/12/americas-changing-religious-landscape/.

(6) Greater Good. "5 Ways Giving Is Good for You." December 13, 2010. https://greatergood.berkeley.edu/article/item/5_ways_giving_is_good_for_you.

(7) Czeisler, Mark É. "Mental Health, Substance Use, and Suicidal Ideation During The . . ." *MMWR. Morbidity and Mortality Weekly Report* 69 (December 29, 2020). https://doi.org/10.15585/mmwr.mm6932a1.

(8) Otterman, Sharon, and Hannah Dreyfus. "Michael Steinhardt, a Leader in Jewish Philanthropy, Is Accused of a Pattern of Sexual Harassment." *The New York Times*, March 21, 2019. https://www.nytimes.com/2019/03/21/nyregion/michael-steinhardt-sexual-harassment.html?

(9) Kampeas, Ron. "After Allegations against Michael Steinhardt, Beneficiaries Are Not Eager to Talk." *Jewish Telegraphic Agency*, March 22, 2019. https://www.jta.org/2019/03/22/united-states/after-allegations-against-michael-steinhardt-beneficiaries-are-not-eager-to-talk?

(10) Staff, JTA. "Sheila Katz, Hillel Executive and Steinhardt Accuser, to Head National Council of Jewish Women." *Jewish Telegraphic Agency*, March 27, 2019. https://www.jta.org/quick-reads/sheila-katz-hillel-executive-and-steinhardt-accuser-to-head-national-council-of-jewish-women?

Chapter 2

(1) Lauterbach, Brian. "The Four Year-End Donor Personas, Reasons They Give & Channels to Reach Them." Bloomerang, November 26, 2019. https://bloomerang.co/blog/the-four-year-end-donor-personas-reasons-they-give-channels-to-reach-them/.

(2) Greater Good. "5 Ways Giving Is Good for You." May 22, 2023. https://greatergood.berkeley.edu/article/item/5_ways_giving_is_good_for_you.

(3) "Definition of Old-School." May 22, 2023. https://www.merriam-webster.com/dictionary/old-school.

(4) Vocabulary.com Dictionary, s.v. "archaic," June 12, 2023, https://www.vocabulary.com/dictionary/archaic.

(5) Kim, Laura. "2020 Findings from the Diary of Consumer Payment Choice." *Federal Reserve Bank of San Francisco*, July 31, 2020. https://www.frbsf.org/cash/publications/fed-notes/2020/july/2020-findings-from-the-diary-of-consumer-payment-choice/.

(6) Fundraise Up. "Payment Methods." May 22, 2023. https://fundraiseup.com/payment-methods/.

(7) Waasdorp, Erica. "Take Action Right Away to Improve Your Monthly Donor Retention." *NonProfit PRO*, March 26, 2018. https://www.nonprofitpro.com/post/take-action-right-away-improve-monthly-donor-retention/.

Chapter 3

(1) Toyne, Gary. "Alumni Access", VAESE Alumni Benchmarking Study.," 2020.

(2) Screen, Steven. "How You Can Use the 80/20 Rule to Raise More Money." *The Better Fundraising Company*, September 29, 2020. https://betterfundraising.com/how-you-can-use-the-80-20-rule/.

(3) Blankenship, Lacie. "New Research Finds Public Recognition Can Decrease Charitable Giving Rates." *Vanderbilt Business*, November 1, 2021. https://business.vanderbilt.edu/news/2021/11/01/new-research-finds-public-recognition-can-decrease-charitable-giving-rates/.

(4) Safranek, Sofia. "Still Publishing Donor Names? Ditch the List." *Blue Avocado*, July 12, 2021. https://blueavocado.org/fundraising/still-publishing-donor-names-ditch-the-list/.

(5) Independent Sector. "Trust in Civil Society 2022 Report," May 19, 2022. https://independentsector.org/resource/trust-in-civil-society/.

(6) Independent Sector. "Trust in Civil Society 2022 Report," May 19, 2022. https://independentsector.org/resource/trust-in-civil-society/.

(7)   The Trust Project. "Kellogg School of Management." May 22, 2023. https://www.kellogg.northwestern.edu/trust-project/videos/waytz-ep-2.aspx.

(8)   Jaffe, Dennis. "The Essential Importance Of Trust: How To Build It Or Restore It." *Forbes*, December 5, 2018. https://www.forbes.com/sites/dennisjaffe/2018/12/05/the-essential-importance-of-trust-how-to-build-it-or-restore-it/?sh=d06664fe5661.

Chapter 4

(1)   Brower, Tracy. "Empathy Is The Most Important Leadership Skill According To Research." *Forbes*, September 19, 2021. https://www.forbes.com/sites/tracybrower/2021/09/19/empathy-is-the-most-important-leadership-skill-according-to-research/?sh=2664be0b3dc5.

(2)   Stembridge, Garret. "Confronting Mental Health Crisis Stemming from the COVID-19 Pandemic." *Qualtrics*, April 14, 2020. https://www.qualtrics.com/blog/confronting-mental-health/.

(3)   Wyatt Koma, Sarah True, Jeannie Fuglesten Biniek, Juliette Cubanski, Kendal Orgera, and Rachel Garfield/ KFF. "One in Four Older Adults Report Anxiety or Depression Amid the COVID-19 Pandemic," October 9, 2020. https://www.kff.org/medicare/issue-brief/one-in-four-older-adults-report-anxiety-or-depression-amid-the-covid-19-pandemic/.

(4)   Brower, Tracy, "Empathy Is The Most Important Leadership Skill According To Research." *Forbes*, September 19, 2021. https://www.forbes.com/sites/tracybrower/2021/09/19/empathy-is-the-most-important-leadership-skill-according-to-research/?sh=7624743e3dc5.

(5)   Greenstein, Jeff. "There's No Debate – Philanthropy Can Be Both Strategic and Empathetic." *Thrive Global*, October 23, 2019. https://community.thriveglobal.com/philanthropy-can-be-both-strategic-and-empathetic/.

(6)   Raimonde, Olivia. "There Are More than 600,000 Millennial Millionaires in the US, According to Report." *CNBC*, October 16, 2019. https://www.cnbc.com/2019/10/16/us-has-more-than-600000-millennial-millionaires-according-to-report.html.

(7)   Brooks, Jeff. "8 Assumptions You Should Make about Donors." *Future Fundraising Now*. October 7, 2020. https://www.futurefundraisingnow.com/future-fundraising/2020/10/8-assumptions-you-should-make-about-donors.html.

(8)   Brooks, Jeff. "Stupid Ad Imagines Donors Look like Dead Bodies." *Future Fundraising Now*. October 4, 2010. https://www.futurefundraisingnow.

com/future-fundraising/2010/10/stupid-ad-imagines-donors-look-like-dead-bodies.html.

Chapter 5

(1) Encyclopedia.com. "Hygiene." May 23, 2023. https://www.encyclopedia.com/medicine/divisions-diagnostics-and-procedures/medicine/hygiene.

(2) Federal Trade Commission. "CAN-SPAM Act: A Compliance Guide for Business," September 2, 2009. https://www.ftc.gov/business-guidance/resources/can-spam-act-compliance-guide-business.

(3) Clairification. "Transform Annual Reports into Gratitude Reports for the Best ROI," January 20, 2023. https://clairification.com/2023/01/19/transform-annual-reports-into-gratitude-reports-for-the-best-roi/.

(4) Independent Sector. "Health of the US Nonprofit Sector," December 31, 2022. https://independentsector.org/wp-content/uploads/2023/01/Quarterly-Health-Report-December-2022_Release-January-2023.pdf.

(5) Indiana University Lilly Family School of Philanthropy. "The Giving Environment: Understanding the Pre-Pandemic Trends in Charitable Giving," July 2021. https://scholarworks.iupui.edu/bitstream/handle/1805/26290/giving-environment210727.pdf

(6) Olson, Nancy. "Five Reasons To Write Thank-You Notes." *Forbes*, January 22, 2017. https://www.forbes.com/sites/nancyolson/2017/01/22/five-reasons-to-write-thank-you-notes/?sh=1e69ba7f2811.

(7) Giving Thanks. "Nonprofit Knowledge Matters." May 23, 2023. https://www.councilofnonprofits.org/civicrm/mailing/view?id=1755.

(8) "Folding@home – Fighting Disease with a World Wide Distributed Super Computer." May 23, 2023. https://foldingathome.org/?lng=en.

Chapter 6

(1) Contributors to Wikimedia projects. "Salon (Gathering)." Wikipedia, March 19, 2023. https://en.wikipedia.org/wiki/Salon_(gathering).

(2) Garry, Joan. "10 Rules for a Successful Small Fundraiser." *Joan Garry Consulting*, December 2, 2013. https://www.joangarry.com/plan-successful-small-fundraiser-donor-event/.

(3) Thorpe, Devin. "How To Organize The Perfect Fundraising Gala." *Forbes*, August 29, 2018. https://www.forbes.com/sites/devinthorpe/2018/08/29/how-to-organize-the-perfect-fundraising-gala/?sh=76b9759379df.

Chapter 7

(1) Gose, Ben. "Why and How Charities Should Revive a Declining but Vital Resource . . . Volunteers." *The Chronicle of Philanthropy*, September 7, 2022. https://www.philanthropy.com/article/why-and-how-charities-should-revive-a-declining-but-vital-resource-volunteers.

(2) Volunteer Recruiting Research. "VolunteerMatch." May 23, 2023. https://www.volunteermatch.org/nonprofits/resources/research.jsp.

(3) Fidelity Charitable. "Time and Money: The Role of Volunteering in Philanthropy." May 23, 2023. https://www.fidelitycharitable.org/insights/volunteering-and-philanthropy.html.

(4) Justis, Jane Leighty. "Why Invest in Volunteer Engagement?" Exponent Philanthropy, October 5, 2021. https://www.exponentphilanthropy.org/blog/why-invest-in-volunteer-engagement/.

(5) Points of Light. "Points of Light," March 19, 2017. https://www.pointsoflight.org/.

(6) Herschander, Sara. "Nonprofit Leaders Want More Volunteers but Say It Is Tough to Recruit Them." *The Chronicle of Philanthropy*, February 7, 2023. https://www.philanthropy.com/article/nonprofit-leaders-want-more-volunteers-but-say-it-is-tough-to-recruit-them?

(7) Burger, Eric. "40 Volunteer Statistics That Will Blow Your Mind." VolunteerHub, November 9, 2021. https://www.volunteerhub.com/blog/40-volunteer-statistics/.

(8) New York Society of Association Executives (NYSAE). "Study Examines Volunteerism and Donations." May 23, 2023. https://www.nysaenet.org/resources1/inviewnewsletter/archives/2009/december2009/inview122009_article7.

(9) Track It Forward. "Why Adult Volunteers Quit And What You Can Do To Prevent Them Quitting." May 23, 2023. https://www.trackitforward.com/content/why-adult-volunteers-quit-and-what-you-can-do-prevent-them-quitting.

(10) The Stelter Company/ Selzer Company. "Discovering the Secret Giver." *Stelter.com*, 2018. https://www.stelter.com/Documents/pdf/industry-research/DiscoveringtheSecretGiver.pdf.

Chapter 8

(1) Mansfield, Heather. "[DATA] 11 Must-Know Stats About Online Fundraising." *Nonprofit Tech for Good* (blog), September 13, 2021. https://

www.nptechforgood.com/2021/09/13/data-11-must-know-stats-about-online-fundraising/.

(2) Donor Perfect. "Monthly Donor Metrics Every Nonprofit Should Know," n.d. https://uploads.donorperfect.com/pdf/Monthly-Donor-Metrics-ebook.pdf.

(3) Mansfield, Heather. "5 Must-Know Recurring Giving Stats for Nonprofit Fundraisers." *Nonprofit Tech for Good* (blog), September 20, 2018. https://www.nptechforgood.com/2018/09/20/5-must-know-recurring-giving-stats-for-nonprofit-fundraisers/.

(4) "Definition of Mensch." May 23, 2023. https://www.merriam-webster.com/dictionary/mensch.

(5) Network for Good. "What Is Recurring Giving? A Guide to Recurring Donations," February 4, 2022. https://www.networkforgood.com/resource/why-recurring-giving-matters/.

(6) Network for Good. "What Is Recurring Giving? A Guide to Recurring Donations," February 4, 2022. https://www.networkforgood.com/resource/why-recurring-giving-matters/.

Chapter 9

(1) Fabry, Merrill. "Now You Know: What Was the First Credit Card?" *Time*, October 19, 2016. https://time.com/4512375/first-credit-card/.

(2) Osterland, Andrew. "Donating a Car to Charity? You Might Want to Pump the Brakes." *CNBC*, November 22, 2017. https://www.cnbc.com/2017/11/21/donating-a-car-to-charity-you-might-want-to-pump-the-brakes.html.

(3) Kumar, Raynil, and Shaun O'Brien. "2019 Findings from the Diary of Consumer Payment Choice." *Federal Reserve Bank of San Francisco*, June 26, 2019. https://www.frbsf.org/cash/publications/fed-notes/2019/june/2019-findings-from-the-diary-of-consumer-payment-choice/.

(4) Cygnus Applied Research. "The Burk Donor Survey." *CYG Research*, December 2019. https://cygresearch.com/wp-content/uploads/2019/12/the-2019-burk-donor-survey-executive-summary.pdf.

Chapter 10

(1) Sharsheret. "Sharsheret - A Jewish Breast Cancer Organization," September 15, 2016. https://sharsheret.org/.

(2) Non Profit News | Nonprofit Quarterly. "Raising Money from Donor-Advised Funds: Navigating Today's Increasingly Complex Philanthropic Landscape - Non Profit News," July 25, 2020. https://nonprofitquarterly.org/raising-money-from-donor-advised-funds-navigating-todays-increasingly-complex-philanthropic-landscape/.

Chapter 11

(1) Ibrisevic, Ilma. "8 Things Your Nonprofit Needs to Know About Online Donors." *Nonprofit Blog*, July 18, 2018. https://donorbox.org/nonprofit-blog/nonprofit-needs-to-know-about-online-donors.

(2) Storyblok. "60% of Consumers Abandon Purchases Due to Poor Website User Experience, Costing E-Commerce Companies Billions," December 15, 2022. https://www.storyblok.com/mp/poor-website-user-experience.

(3) Frank, Tema. "42 Ways To Scare Off Your Customers With Bad Website Design." *Mirasee*, February 16, 2015. https://mirasee.com/blog/bad-website-design/.

(4) Duray, Dan. "When Is a High-Maintenance Donor Not Worth the Trouble?" *Town & Country*, May 20, 2019. https://www.townandcountrymag.com/society/money-and-power/a27309526/donations-with-strings-attached/.

(5) Calvert, Gina. "What the Numbers Say About Recurring Giving." *Vision2* (blog), December 20, 2021. https://vision2.com/blog/what-the-numbers-say-about-recurring-giving.

(6) M+R Benchmarks 2023. "2023 Nonprofit Benchmarks." May 23, 2023. https://mrbenchmarks.com/.

(7) Erdie, Garcelle Vierra, and PNC Bank. "Women, Wealth, and the 'Great Wealth Transfer.'" *AVLtoday*, October 28, 2022. https://avltoday.6amcity.com/women-wealth-and-the-great-wealth-transfer.

(8) National Council of Nonprofits. "Fundraising," June 12, 2023. https://www.councilofnonprofits.org/running-nonprofit/fundraising-and-resource-development/fundraising.

(9) Schulte, Taylor. "80+ Charitable Giving Statistics & Demographics (2023)." *Define Financial*, February 10, 2023. https://www.definefinancial.com/blog/charitable-giving-statistics/.

(10) Joslyn, Heather. "51% of Fundraisers Plan to Leave Their Jobs by 2021, Says New Survey." *The Chronicle of Philanthropy*, August 6, 2019. https://www.philanthropy.com/article/51-of-fundraisers-plan-to-leave-their-jobs-by-2021-says-new-survey/?sra=true&cid=gen_sign_in.

(11) "Fundraisers: Occupational Outlook Handbook:: U.S. Bureau of Labor Statistics," September 8, 2022. https://www.bls.gov/ooh/business-and-financial/fundraisers.htm.

(12) Rosen, Seth. "Fundraisers: Here's How to Avoid Burnout." *Joan Garry Consulting*, March 18, 2015. https://www.joangarry.com/avoid-burnout/.

(13) Marketing Department. "Calculating the Cost of Losing High-Performing Fundraisers." *Grenzebach Glier & Associates Inc.* May 23, 2023. https://www.grenzebachglier.com/2021/06/10/calculating-the-cost-of-losing-high-performing-fundraisers/.

(14) Yours App. "Emotions in the Workplace: Why Managers Need to Care," May 2022. https://yoursapp.com/business/blog/workplace-emotions/.

(15) An earlier version of this article is featured in the AFP's January 2022 edition of Advancing Philanthropy Magazine. Association of Fundraising Professionals. *"Advancing Philanthropy*, January 2022," December 31, 2021. https://afpglobal.org/advancing-philanthropy/advancing-philanthropy-january-2022.

Chapter 12

(1) National Council of Nonprofits. "Board Roles and Responsibilities." May 24, 2023. https://www.councilofnonprofits.org/running-nonprofit/governance-leadership/board-roles-and-responsibilities.

(2) Stanford School of Business/ Rock Center for Corporate Governance. "2015 Survey on Board of Directors of Nonprofit Organizations." *Stanford*, 2015. https://www.gsb.stanford.edu/sites/gsb/files/publication-pdf/cgri-survey-nonprofit-board-directors-2015.pdf.

(3) Usmani, Sameena. "4 Qualities of an Effective Nonprofit Board." *Taproot Foundation*, December 16, 2021. https://taprootfoundation.org/4-qualities-of-an-effective-nonprofit-board/.

(4) Arnwine, Don L. "Effective Governance: The Roles and Responsibilities of Board Members." *Proceedings (Baylor University. Medical Center)* 15, no. 1 (January 1, 2002). https://doi.org/10.1080/08998280.2002.11927809.

(5) Harvard Business Review. "The New Work of the Nonprofit Board," September 1, 1996. https://hbr.org/1996/09/the-new-work-of-the-nonprofit-board.

(6) Taylor, Jim. "Reflections on Trust and Its Relationship to Racial Inequity on Nonprofit Boards." *BoardSource* (blog), May 21, 2020. https://blog.

boardsource.org/blog/reflections-on-trust-and-its-relationship-to-racial-inequity-on-nonprofit-boards.

(7) Coldwell Banker Global Luxury. "A Look at Wealth 2019." *Coldwell Banker Luxury*, 2019. https://blog.coldwellbankerluxury.com/wp-content/uploads/2019/10/CBGL Millennial-Report_SEP19_FINAL-4a.1-1-1.pdf.

(8) Distribution: Distribution of Household Wealth in the U.S. since 1989. "The Fed." May 24, 2023. https://www.federalreserve.gov/releases/z1/dataviz/dfa/distribute/chart/#quarter:129;series:Net%20demographic:generation;population:3,5,7;units:levels;range:2019.4,2021.4.

(9) Choy, Esther. "Transforming Partnerships Between Fundraisers and First Generation Wealth Creators." *Leadership Story Lab*, April 23, 2021. https://www.leadershipstorylab.com/wealth-creators-research/.

Chapter 13

(1) Marshall, Alex. "An Opera Company's Precarious Future Has Some Worried About a Ripple Effect." *The New York Times*, December 9, 2022. https://www.nytimes.com/2022/12/09/arts/music/english-national-opera-future.html.

(2) English National Opera. "Home," December 10, 2015. https://www.eno.org/.

(3) Sahni, Nidhi, Laura Lanzerotti, Amira Bliss, and Daniel Pike. "Is Your Nonprofit Built for Sustained Innovation?" *Stanford Social Innovation Review*, 2017. https://doi.org/10.48558/1JCV-R152.

(4) Huntsberger, Alex. "Year-End Giving Statistics Every Fundraiser Should Know." *Neon One*, November 22, 2022. https://neonone.com/resources/blog/year-end-giving-statistics/.

Chapter 14

(1) Lilly Family School of Philanthropy. "IU Lilly Family School of Philanthropy News," November 3, 2021. https://philanthropy.iupui.edu/news-events/news-item/new-study-provides-insights-into-year-end-and-workplace-giving-in-light-of-shifts-in-philanthropic-environment.html?id=374.

(2) Indiana University Lilly Family School of Philanthropy, "Understanding Philanthropy in Times of Crisis: The Role of Giving Back During COVID-19," n.d. November 2021. https://scholarworks.iupui.edu/bitstream/handle/1805/26934/philanthropy-crisis-nov21.pdf

(3) Non Profit News | Nonprofit Quarterly. "New Data Tells Us Where Donor-Advised Fund Dollars Go—And Don't Go - Non Profit News," April 27, 2022. https://nonprofitquarterly.org/new-data-tells-us-where-donor-advised-fund-dollars-go-and-dont-go/.

(4) Eisen, Ben, and Anne Tergesen. "Older Americans Stockpiled a Record $35 Trillion. The Time Has Come to Give It Away." *The Wall Street Journal*, July 2, 2021. https://www.wsj.com/articles/older-americans-35-trillion-wealth-giving-away-heirs-philanthropy-11625234216?

(5) Ruffenach, Glenn. "How (and Whether) to Give Heirs Their Inheritance Before You Die." *The Wall Street Journal*, March 8, 2020. https://www.wsj.com/articles/a-retiree-choice-give-some-of-it-away-early-11582647993?mod=article_inline.

(6) Fandos, Nicholas. "Connections to a Cause: The Millennial Way of Charity." *The New York Times*, November 3, 2016. https://www.nytimes.com/2016/11/06/giving/connections-to-a-cause-the-millennial-way-of-charity.html.

INDEX